This book is dedicated to you, the reader.

I once felt Heaven whisper in my ear.
Tell women that there is a
God in Heaven and
a company of people here on earth
who believe in them also.

Introduction: The Ultimate Compliment   xi

Part One: People Need Your Story

CHAPTER ONE   Once Upon a Time . . .   5

CHAPTER TWO   Stories to Learn From   13

CHAPTER THREE   My Story   21

Part Two: Break the Containment

CHAPTER FOUR   "I'm Inadequate"; "I Can't";   35
                   "I Have Nothing to Give"

CHAPTER FIVE   Confront the Containment   44

CHAPTER SIX   Mindsets, Enemies,   55
                   and Spiritual Blindness

Part Three: Negotiate Your Journey Well

CHAPTER SEVEN   Recognize the Challenge   73

CHAPTER EIGHT   Recognize the Real Enemy   85

CHAPTER NINE   Guard the Specifics   96

Part Four: Be a Woman of Strong Conviction

CHAPTER TEN   Conviction, Calling, and the Cause   111

CHAPTER ELEVEN   Hold Your Ground; Don't Give It Away   116

CHAPTER TWELVE   Conviction that Produces   121

CONTENTS

Part Five: Be a Woman of Strong Resolve

CHAPTER THIRTEEN   Don't Settle for Half a Testimony   133
CHAPTER FOURTEEN   Become an Agent of Resolve   137
CHAPTER FIFTEEN   Birth Something Big and Beautiful   141

Part Six: Be a Woman of Strong Partnership

CHAPTER SIXTEEN   Partner with Your Own Vision   149
CHAPTER SEVENTEEN   Partner with the One to Whom   153
You Said "I Do"
CHAPTER EIGHTEEN   Partner with the Master Plan   161

Epilogue: Color Your World Beautiful!   169
About the Author   175

Always Grateful

I wish to acknowledge and give honor where
honor is due . . .

To Brian, I am so glad we fell in love! Thank you for being a
faithful and loyal husband, father, and partner in life. Thank you
for shaping our world into what it is today.

To the three most generous, loving, and accommodating children—Joel, Ben, and Laura. Whatever did we do to deserve you
handsome three?

To faithful, loyal, and true friends who love us who are a con-
stant source of encouragement and inspiration!

To "our" parents, Frank and Hazel Houston and Doreen and
Arthur McDonald, for depositing your best into us. We honor you.

To the greatest church on the planet—Hillsong Church! You
are simply the best. God put us all together and then He stamped
us with blessing and favor. Isn't that amazing? I praise the team
alongside us who work with such devotion and diligence to
achieve the dream. They own it as passionately as we do.

And to the love of my life—to a Heavenly Father who considered and loved me before the foundations of the earth. To Jesus
Christ for knocking loud and clear on the door of my heart and
then drawing me unto Himself; and to the dear Holy Spirit, who
I am discovering is the perfect Helper, Travelling Companion,
and Friend.

COMP
con

the ul

LIMENT

liment

'I'll have what she's having!
Could it be **the ultimate Compliment?**'

\Com"pli*ment\, n.
1. expression of praise; act implying praise
2. pay compliment to (person or thing)

nate compliment

Phoebe (photo by Rachael Sadler)

The Ultimate Compliment

Who can forget that famous scene in the 1989 movie *When Harry Met Sally* when actress Meg Ryan simulated a climatic moment in a crowded cafe? The response, "I'll have what she's having!" from an envious female onlooker inspired the title of this book. Perhaps your response is similar to my dear husband's response: "Bobbie, you can't be serious, you can't call a book that!"

But I did.

"I'll have what she's having!" Could it be the ultimate compliment? Could it be the most *rewarding* compliment a person might receive? That someone else would observe your lifestyle, attitude, sense of purpose, resolve, and conviction, and then desire the same in their own life? I personally do believe it is the ultimate compliment and also a *mandate* that belongs to every Christian woman, young or mature, regardless of whether she is in actual leadership or not.

I chose to write this not because I think I have all the answers.

I certainly do not pretend to know it all because I am also still on my journey of life and discovery, but I write it for two reasons.

Many years ago, as my husband Brian and I began our journey in ministry, we attended a conference where I encountered a beautiful young woman in the bathroom who exclaimed, "I'd hate to be a pastor's wife!" This response and attitude was not uncommon back then and I can only surmise that somewhere, some pastor's wife had left a very unpleasant taste in this young woman's mouth.

At the time, my heart was greatly saddened. In what was really only a very brief encounter, I remember reflecting, *I am also a young woman. I am a young pastor's wife. I am new to the things of God and new to the things of ministry. The entire journey of marriage and motherhood is just beginning for me.* Yet upon hearing that comment, something almost rose within me and cried, *Dear Lord, please help me to live my life in such a way that no woman ever looks at me and says, "I'd hate to be her. I'd hate to be in the ministry. I'd hate to be in leadership."* That's the first reason.

The second reason occurred to me at the close of one of our annual Hillsong Leadership Conferences in Sydney, Australia. Countless men and women came and thanked me and Brian, our team, and our church for standing strong and firm. They thanked us for our openness, honesty, and transparency. I realized we had shared truths that could help others overcome. We are always humbled by such response to our ministry, and without hesitation give God the glory because where would any of us be without His grace? However, isn't this what leadership and ministry is really about? People are not going to look at our lives and comment, "I'll have what they're having" or "I'll have what she's having" if our lives reflect insecurity, defeat, and hopelessness.

Every woman who declares that Jesus Christ is her Lord and Savior should reflect—or be in the process of learning to reflect— a life of confidence, victory, blessing, fulfillment, and destiny. Yes— every woman! That's you, girl! The Amplified Bible magnificently describes the person who is "blessed" as one who is "happy, fortunate and to be envied" (Gen. 30:13). That means we ought to be blessed and happy. We ought to be experiencing a fortunate and prosperous life, and we ought to be enviable in the purest sense.

I pray with all my heart that the time God gives me on this planet will reflect the goodness of my incredible Savior. I pray that the gorgeous women, the young and the mature, that God has entrusted into our care and spiritual stewardship will look at my life and want what is in me. Not that they will see Bobbie Houston, but rather "Bobbie Houston in Christ"—smiling at life, succeeding, enjoying, and fulfilling her God-given potential and destiny. I hope that these thoughts and the Truth found in God's Word will bless and inspire you to become the awesome woman that God has designed you to be.

Before we go any further, let me share something with you. You, dear friend, whoever you are and wherever you are, are *precious, priceless,* and *extremely important* to an amazing God in Heaven. He knows your name, He sees your life, and He cares about the inner desires of your heart.

Perhaps you are new to the things of God and are just stepping into the wonderful world of serving Him. Be encouraged because you are not alone and you can reach for the sky and accomplish things beyond your wildest dreams. Perhaps you are seasoned in this journey and are faithfully pressing on to achieve God's purposes. I have affinity with you and believe that together we can impact this planet with God's goodness. Perhaps you have run well, but are now feeling weary, unappreciated, and your heart is saying, "It's not worth it." Please allow me to speak into your life as a friend and remind you that *it is worth it!* Or perhaps someone has placed this book in your hand and the thought of Christian women being dynamic is a foreign concept to you. Stay with me and allow me the privilege of revealing a world beyond your wildest dreams.

If you love God and know this beautiful Jesus as your Savior, then I challenge you to run after Him with everything that is within you. We are living in truly exciting and significant days where, as He promised in His Word, He is pouring out His Spirit in unprecedented ways. Not a minute is to be wasted. If, however, you find yourself distant or removed from your Creator, then I lovingly encourage you to do as it says in James 4:8: "Draw near to God and He will draw near to you" (NASB). Open your heart right now and allow Jesus Christ, the ultimate lover of humanity, access into your life. It is time to rise up, push those lovely shoulders back, lift that beautiful chin, and become the delightful Daughter of God that you already are.

My objective in putting pen to paper is that anyone reading this will fall more in love with Jesus and more in love with life! Nothing more; nothing less. To love God is to discover your Creator and your created purpose, and to love life is to live that life to its fullest. In achieving these objectives alone, you will discover your designed purpose for this sojourn on earth, and you will discover a personal satisfaction beyond your wildest imaginations. So stay with me and follow my heart. I pray that reading this will be an enjoyable experience—I certainly have had fun living it thus far.

PART 1

PEOPLE NEED
YOUR STORY

'**Your story** (or testimony) can bring wisdom and life to the people you meet along the way.'

people

\Sto'ry\, n.
1. a narrative; tale; account of a journey travelled
2. facts or experiences that deserve narration

STORY

need your story

'ONE GENERATION
shall praise Your works to another,
and shall declare Your mighty acts'

{ PSALM 145:4 }

CHAPTER ONE

Once Upon a Time . . .

People need your story! Never be tempted to limit "Once upon a time . . ." to only fairytale settings. Once upon a time, you were planned, designed, conceived, and arrived on the planet in the perfect timing and purpose of Almighty God. God has His story, the greatest ever told, but every single human being who has ever walked this earth and breathed its sweet air also has a story.

Life is a journey. It has a beginning and an end, and everything that happens along the way becomes your story. Unfortunately, many people fail to travel within the safe parameters of wisdom and they end up with a tale of distances traveled that is less successful and fulfilling than was intended. This may have been through personal choice or ignorance, or it may have been imposed on them by circumstances beyond their control. Others, however, enjoy a smoother journey because they framed their lives with the more successful principles of right living. Whatever the scenario, your story—your experience—is valuable, and it has the capacity to make a difference in this world.

All of us have negatives things to deal with in our lives, but once dealt with and overcome, these negatives become powerful tools that can bring inspiration, healing, deliverance, and restoration to others. For example, insecurity was a major negative that contained me for a long time; however I know that my story (or my testimony) of overcoming this insecurity has been a source of blessing to others, giving them courage to also overcome. Those who know me well have watched and thought, *If Bobbie can do it, so can we!*

Become a Source of Inspiration to Others

I want to encourage you to reflect upon your own story. Dare to believe that your past, your present, and yes, even your future, can actually bring inspiration to others.

King David, a man whose heart leapt within him because of his powerful relationship with God wrote, "The law of the LORD is perfect, converting the soul: the testimony of the LORD is sure, making wise the simple" (Ps. 19:7). I love these verses. As I understand them, the "law of the LORD" is the Word of God, which paints wisdom across your journey and experience. The "testimony of the LORD" is the wonderful story of God at work in your life—it is strong and sure, and bears testimony to God's amazing grace at work in us. And "making wise the simple" is the revelation and reality that your story (or your testimony) can bring wisdom and life to the people you may meet along the way.

An incident comes to mind that illustrates this perfectly. A number of years ago I was a guest speaker at a women's meeting—a meeting that was hard work at the time, but now is funny upon reflection. The meeting was held in a hotel tavern on a Friday evening. The manager promised our host an undisturbed function room, but when I arrived, this gathering of lovely Christian women was sharing the room with the equally lovely, but somewhat intoxicated, Friday night patrons. Nothing but a flimsy partition separated us from the loud music, smoke, and pub atmosphere.

I must confess, when I walked in and surveyed the scene, peace and serenity were not my portion! Negativity and panic momentarily gripped me and I found myself silently mouthing to God, "This is not going to work!" But the meeting was handed over to me and I began. Now because of the level of volume from behind the thin partition, I had to raise my voice to be heard. Well, the louder I went, the louder they turned up the volume. My "highly anointed" passage from Isaiah was contending with music from . . . would you believe this? . . . *Phantom of the Opera!* The louder I got, the louder the Phantom got!

And then, to cap the night off, the table of delightful ladies at the very rear of the room was rudely "brown-eyed"—*mooned,* that is—by a bunch of men obviously under the influence. I must admit I am glad I didn't witness that bizarre moment, and I take my hat off to those poor women who endured the opposition that was happening at the back of the meeting. However God is good (all the time!) and the message miraculously got through. But what I remember most about that evening is the lovely woman who approached me afterwards and told me her story.

She had lived a very restricted life and had not been given a lot of opportunity. She had not been given the choice to be educated, had made some wrong choices, and consequently experienced feelings of inadequacy and uselessness. But somewhere along the line, God got hold of her (or rather she took hold of God) and she made some positive choices, deciding not to remain in this defeated state. In her late thirties, she went back to full-time study and was heading toward a career in welfare. Her dream was to help those less fortunate in life.

What I find delightful about this woman's story is that her tenacity and courage to change her circumstances had given her friends to do the same. This woman could have stayed contained, but she is now a leader among women, giving courage and strength to others to do likewise.

Christine's Story

I have a friend whose "Once upon a time . . ." story greatly inspires me. She is a spirited, talented young woman with the hand of God richly upon her—a woman who God is using magnificently to point people all over the planet to Him.

Her passion for life and her passion to serve God are all consuming, and even a little intimidating. But I know Christine's story—her background, her obstacles, her abuse, and the enemies she has confronted—and how she has defeated those things to become who she is today. When Christine shares her incredible story, women are inspired and realize that if they have had any excuses for not standing up and becoming the women they were created to be, those excuses are shattered.

This young lady has every reason on the planet not to achieve, yet because Christ is in her, He is the hope of glory in her life, and

Christ is the grace that has picked her up, healed her, and set her on course. She has risen above and plundered every excuse. Hers is a testimony of true inspiration and true leadership—it is a story to be shared and shouted from the rooftops.

The reality is that *you* also have a story to tell! Perhaps it is just beginning. Perhaps it has been a long time in the making. Perhaps you've shelved it because it has become too hard or difficult. Be encouraged. As I said before, dare to believe and even become excited that your story can bring hope and encouragement to others. This is what leadership and the kingdom of God is about.

God's nature is to give. His first priority is to bring life, hope, and encouragement to us. His desire is that we then will carry that same life, hope, and encouragement to others. God smiles when He observes us living our lives with this same unselfish spirit of generosity, so that wherever our cute little feet take us, we are freely giving to others all that we have learned along the way.

Before his own conversion, the awesome apostle Paul was a crazy, radical, zealot who hated God's people and sought to harass or murder them (see Acts 9:1). He got fabulously saved, showing that there is hope for the very worst. Under the influence of the Holy Spirit, he penned much wisdom and instruction to you and me, often likening the story of life to a race.

Never Alone in the Race of Life

In the book written to the Hebrews, we are encouraged that we are definitely not alone in our race (see Heb. 12). Life positions us with people who are either running alongside us, in front of us or behind us. I am sure if Paul or any of our forerunners could speak to us now, they'd be like big brothers. They would possibly say it like this:

"Girls, listen up. You are definitely not alone in this race of life. For starters, we are all watching you from heaven. I know that's a wild concept, but it's true. Now, if that isn't enough to make you feel secure at night, Jesus (the awesome One who is the Author, the Source, and the Finisher of all our individual races) is watching too. Does that connect in your brain? Jesus is watching! Does that make you feel better?

Heaven wants you to run the race well. Want some advice? Lose the sin—it messes everything up. Shake off the stuff from the past. Jesus paid a big price so you could do that, and set your eyes on the finish line. However, do not forget you are supposed to do a few things along the way. Become Christ-like, become true daughters, and gather people as you go. Heaven goes crazy when you bring people to Christ. And this is really important—run with your eyes open and watch out for one another because we do not want anyone to miss out on heaven's mega-party. We are all madly excited about it. Have you sent your RSVP yet? In the meantime, get good at all this stuff. Wise up! Take note of everything, and we'll watch you bring heaven to earth as the twenty-first century unfolds."

My imagination runs away with me sometimes; I hope you can cope with it. Nevertheless, here are these verses from Hebrews 12 (the Amplified Bible version, not the Bobbie version, although I have inserted some comments in parentheses below). They are very good, so do not skip over them. (*Hey, we all get tempted to skip or skim read the Bible bits, but the Bible bits are the best bits—they're the bits that change us.*)

So then, brace up and reinvigorate and set right your slackened and weakened and drooping hands and strengthen your feeble and palsied and tottering knees *(imagine running the race of life in this condition?)*, And cut through and make firm and plain and smooth, straight paths for your feet [yes, make them] safe and upright and happy paths that go in the right direction *(strong, happy paths that have people saying, "I'll have what she's having")*, so that the lame and halting [limbs] may not be put out of joint, but rather may be cured. *(These are the people we are supposed to gather along the way, because of our awesome testimony.)* Strive to live in peace with everybody and pursue that consecration and holiness without which no one will [ever] see the Lord. *(This is an amazing challenge. I think we should all take notice.)* Exercise foresight and be on the watch to look [after one another], to see that no one falls back from and fails to secure God's grace . . . " *(very, very important—keep your eyes open and watch for everyone running in front, behind, and alongside you so that no one misses out on God's grace and answers)*. (Heb. 12:12 – 15, with my comments)

God passionately wants our "Once upon a time . . ." to be a success story. He wants us to "run our race well" so our success and victory can be a blessing to others. In this journey of life, God would have us all participating. No one is supposed to be sitting in the grandstands, observing, criticizing, or asleep. No one is supposed to be sitting muddied and hurt on the sideline. We are all to be pressing forward, understanding that Jesus Christ is the individual prize for all of us. The above verses tell us that the Lord would have each of us gathering as many people as we can along the way. The word of our testimony and the power of our story is what will win them over to the abundant life Christ has for us all.

And may we never forget that there will always be those ahead of us. They're in front, not because they are more gifted or talented, but simply because they are further advanced in their journey. Our attitude, as one following, should always be to cheer them on and encourage them that we are following hard on their heels. Then of course, should we find ourselves in the lead, our attitude is that we would be wise leaders to those following us. Leadership is very much about carrying a story marked with integrity and stewardship.

Perhaps you can think of people alongside you that are an inspiration. If so, fantastic! Or perhaps you may feel like you have no one in your life like this. Do not be discouraged; just keep reading, because God's desire is to connect you with a multitude of people from whose lives you can glean.

CHAPTER TWO

Stories to Learn From

ne of the great benefits of being a believer planted in an alive, vibrant, and healthy church is that you are positioned among wonderful people from whom you can learn and observe. I am ever grateful that since the moment I met Jesus, His grace has surrounded me with such people. Insecurity has not distanced or robbed me of their examples, and their wonderful spirits have truly encouraged me to reach for more in my life. My mother-in-law was a perfect example of an older godly woman who discovered what it was to be content and serve God with an uncompromising passion.

Hazel's Story

Hazel Houston was the precious one who had the privilege of shattering my naive perception of what a pastor's wife should look like. Sadly, too many still hold to an archaic perception of Christian women, and ministers' wives in particular. They often only see them as drab, colorless, lack-luster women who never smile or laugh, and who do not know how to enjoy life, love, intimacy, and anything else that seems remotely enjoyable. It is an image that has the unconverted world saying, "I definitely *do not* want what they're having!"

In my naivety, I thought all pastors' wives were meek and mild, quiet and demure, extremely petite. Mind you, I was only seventeen, and had only observed one pastor's wife, so my worldview was a little narrow. The morning I met Hazel is an experience I will never forget!

Brian had driven me four hundred miles south from Auckland to Wellington to meet his family. (That drive is another story. I was so shy that I wouldn't ask him for a bathroom-stop. Consequently, four hundred miles later, my bladder was full nearly up to my eyeballs. Anyway, back to Hazel.) We knocked on the back door and Hazel responded. She flung open the back door and there stood this wild woman! Apron-clad, covered in flour, barefoot, and not what you might call petite, she was catering that morning for her daughter's wedding. Where was meek, mild, quiet, and demure?

What I most admired in this woman of God, thirty-six years my senior and thirty-six years more advanced in the journey, was that she was a spirited woman who never denied her God. Despite extreme criticism and obstacles that accompanied her generation, Hazel stood strong beside her partner and faithfully served God and His kingdom. She was a woman who did not allow incorrect perceptions to squeeze her into a mould that denied who she truly was, and she was a woman prepared to forsake all to follow a dream and destiny. I truly believe that when she met her Creator she heard, "Well done Hazel, you did very well."

In her final days as an eighty-year-old woman, she remained active, was always laughing, and stayed true to her dreams. She was the first to tell you that her world had not been without its challenges, but then who among us lives in a perfect world? What a lovely example to aspire to. We all need strong women out in front, leading the charge, and I challenge you to become such a woman. If Hazel could do it, so can you and I.

Donna's Story

Who else inspires me? A longtime friend called Donna Crouch. Donna faithfully led our youth group for six years, and now sits on our executive team, overseeing strategic areas in the life of Hillsong Church. She now is doing a wonderful job in the community arm of our church, reaching out to the broken and hurting in our city.

When Donna became a Christian, she was a horse-loving hippie, hanging around a part of Australia that was very "alternative." Despite a university background, she was shy and insecure, so even praying grace around a dinner table was a major challenge for her. Today she is a stunning woman, wife, and mother, with singular vision and a capacity for God's kingdom that is quite breathtaking. Whenever she stands and ministers, it is never without warmth, compassion, authority, and a genuine desire for people to secure God's best for their lives. She is totally beautiful and I often watch her and pray, *Dear Lord, please give me a spirit like hers.*

You see, it is that very spirit and servant heart that has brought Donna continual promotion with much responsibility. She openly loves God and has literally laid down her life for the kingdom. I say that not because it sounds noble, but rather because it is a life-changing truth that has borne much fruit in her life.

We witnessed Donna devote her twenties to building and serving our youth group. She put aside her own desires, relationships, and possessions to sow herself into a bunch of pimply-faced, gorgeous, radical, potential-laden young people, and now I see the Father rewarding her diligence and selfless commitment. She is married to a great man, has three delightful children, a beautiful home, a sense of completeness, and is highly esteemed and honored by others. I might also add that the majority of those potential-laden young people have become awesome young adults and are an integral part of the strength of our church today.

But, do you know what I find even greater about Donna? The girl is not content to settle down. She's still pressing on, and as a team player in our church, she is always open to new horizons and challenges. What an example, what an exceptional lady, you might say. Yes, she is! If God can accomplish much through her, He can certainly do it through you and me.

Darlene's Story

Who else shall I write about? My life is actually full of awesome women who inspire not only me, but many others as well. Darlene Zschech is one worthy of mention, because she is a lady who has come to an impacting awareness of why she was created. She will gently tell you, "I was created to worship," and it is this simple heart-passion that makes her one of the finest and most influential worship leaders in the world today.

The miracle and dynamic of Darlene's life is that her magnificent example has and will continue to unearth, inspire, and lead thousands of other like-spirited worship leaders around this world. Together, a sound from heaven is arising on the earth that is making this crazy world sit up and take notice!

The woman is uncomplicated. Oh, the potential to be complicated is there; like all of us, Darlene has her story, but she is another example of an overcoming spirit. She is passionately committed, and this is a great quality because Jesus actually told us to lay our lives down for the kingdom. She is gorgeous, feminine, and beautiful in her role as a wife and mother, and daily this young woman is becoming more like Jesus. What more could we ask for? I love this woman and so many aspects of her life cheer me on.

Become a Story of Grace

Isn't this race amazing? We are all in it. Can you believe me when I encourage you that you have a story to tell? If you have negatives in your life that are containing you, get over them and let your story have a voice. Why? Because there are women in this race who need the wisdom and the victory of your testimony. There are women in your world that I may never touch— Donna, Darlene, Christine, and Hazel may never touch them—but you will.

I also want to acknowledge and honor a number of great women friends who, despite broken dreams, tragedy, collapsed relationships, and seeming failures, have risen to stand tall. Their testimonies have given, and continue to give, immeasurable courage to many. In our church, we lovingly call these women "trophies of grace." Where would they be had Jesus not lifted them from their brokenness? Actually, where would any of us be if it were not for Jesus?

Life is not without challenges and enemies, but God calls and enables us to be "overcomers." At the moment of rebirth, when you give your life to Christ, the label "overcomer" does not suddenly appear on your chest. That would be fabulous, but it just doesn't happen. The reason life has challenges and can sometimes appear unkind is that, since the day of Adam's fall, Light and Darkness have been engaged in warfare. God is not mean, unkind, or inattentive to our lives—humanity just happens to live in a fallen state. We turn into overcomers as we engage life and its challenges and emerge with victory under our belts. The final book in the Bible says, "They overcame [Satan] by the blood of the lamb and the word of their testimony" (Rev. 12:11 NIV). A powerful partnership exists where you and Christ work together, and then because of His truly amazing grace, we each emerge with a story to tell.

Your Story Doesn't Have to Be Average

I was once told that over the course of a lifetime, the average person encounters approximately ten thousand people. This phenomenal number can apparently involve anything from a nod or greeting with a stranger to a complete relationship with someone. When you are involved in leadership and/or church life, the borders or parameters of your life are not average and that figure greatly multiplies. Your life has the amazing capacity and potential to touch countless people because of the ever-increasing nature of God's kingdom.

Christ has done and continues to do a unique and powerful work in you. It cost Christ His life to redeem you, and right now He stands in heaven praying that the good work He began in you will be completed (Phil. 1:6). He longs for that good thing to become a story, a voice, and a testimony in the earth that will lead others into similar lives of freedom.

You have probably gathered that I am very excited about your potential. This is the very reason Brian and I, and our friends, do what we do. We lie awake at night, we labor when we do not have to, we resist mediocrity, and we are prepared to live on the edge if need be, because we believe so passionately in the potential of God's people. I believe your story and the testimony of Christ at work in you can bring wisdom, clarity, and hope to more people than perhaps you realize.

I believe in you! I believe in you! *I believe in you!* And I believe that God wants to do such a magnificent work in you that your life will stop people in their tracks and have them say, "I'll definitely have what she's having!"

Photo by Femia Shirliff

Me and my gorgeous son Joel

{ February 2002 }

CHAPTER THREE

My Story

There is something about the written word that is wonderfully enduring. Not all will find themselves as authors one day, but I hope that most people will discover the value of journaling about their lives. For that reason, let me share a little of my story with you.

I was born in Auckland, New Zealand. My mother was a delicate, gentle woman of Scottish descent with pale white skin and flaming red hair. Toward the end of her life, she became frail and incapacitated, but prior to that my memories are of a placid and softly spoken woman, from whose mouth I cannot ever remember hearing harsh or unkind words. (I wonder if you and I could boast that compliment?) She taught me dressmaking, and only once did I ever see her disagree with my father.

My dad was a truly amazing man. He was of Tongan-Island descent and had that gentle disposition that often marks Pacific Islanders. Totally dedicated to his wife and two girls, he spoilt us rotten. I fell asleep in his lap or reclining on his strong, muscular arms every night of my life, and almost every day of our lives he gave my sister and me breakfast in bed.

My fondest memories are of sitting on the porch with him every afternoon after school. We would share a shandy (beer and lemonade) and homemade chips (wrapped in newspaper) that he had cooked especially for me. He was so lovely. I wish my own children had known him. I do not ever remember him raising his hand or voice to me, which for some people is almost beyond comprehension. His philosophy on children was, "Of course you can spoil (or indulge) children, as long as you spoil them with love."

He died when I was fourteen years old, and my world momentarily fell apart. My memories of him are sweet—big strong hands lifting me as a child to reach the ceiling; a daddy who never denied me crawling into bed with them when I was afraid; a man who loved creation and rose at dawn to watch the birds and sunrise; a man who worked hard and diligently; a man who always put others before himself. (Herein lies a challenge for each and every one of us—to create these kind of sweet memories for our children.)

One month before he died, he walked my lovely sister Karen down the aisle and when the minister asked, "Who gives this woman away," he said, "I do, but I want her back!" When he left this world suddenly at sixty-one years of age, I was shattered. He literally was my world.

The reason I speak so strongly and affectionately of my father, Arthur Gordon McDonald, is because he had a profound and powerful effect upon my life. I was blessed to have a truly "perfect" earthly father, which made it very easy for me to comprehend an "even more perfect" Heavenly Father.

There are many women in this crazy, sin-affected world of ours who cannot comprehend their Heavenly Father because they judge God according to what their earthly fathers were like. They were perhaps neglected, abused, and unloved. The reality is that even though they may have been denied such an earthly example, it does not mean they cannot experience, to the fullest and deepest, the love and care of their Heavenly Father. He will never neglect, hurt, or cease from loving any of us.

The Word of God declares that He neither sleeps nor slumbers (Ps. 121:4). He doesn't sleep, which means His eyes are continually toward you and His ears are continually attentive to your cry. The Word says His hand is "not so short that it cannot save" (Isa. 59:1 NASB). He is a covenant-keeping God. What I am writing is truth. The only thing that prevents a beautiful human being from experiencing this amazing gift of love is that person's inability to choose and accept this Truth.

My story is not one of abuse or tragedy (except for a father who died far too early), but I still needed this Heavenly Father. When my dad left this life, this little lady began the process of coming into a knowledge of God. I had lived fourteen great and precious years, but,

- I didn't know Jesus personally,
- I wasn't saved,
- I wasn't walking in my created purpose, and
- I was dissatisfied and hungry for Truth.

Six months after my father's death, I found myself confronted with the Truth of the gospel, and thankfully, Jesus only had to knock once on the door of my heart. One big, clear knock, and as a fifteen-year-old girl I flung open my heart and almost shouted, "Excellent! There You are! I think I've been looking for You!"

My Encounter

On May 7, 1972 in the Auckland Town Hall, I met Jesus Christ, the Son of God. That day, my life, my adventure, and my destiny truly began. The sense of being alone and orphaned from this wonderful Heavenly Father and sense of origin vanished. I still remember being dropped home by the friends who had taken me to church that night. I knocked on the front door, and as my mother opened it, I exclaimed "Mum! I am saved!" She quietly responded, "Oh, that's nice dear." I remember those moments as though they were yesterday. I sat down in the lounge room. The TV was on and although seemingly nothing had happened, I felt distinctly different. I felt clean and forgiven—Someone powerful had entered my life.

I had lived a quiet and sheltered life. I was shy and insecure, and had never really been encouraged to excel or go after anything other than what was normal or expected. Despite having an artistic flare, I chose typing at high school (very handy in retrospect) because that is what my older sister had chosen. When I voiced an interest in music, I was told, "It's just a phase. You'll grow out of it." I never traveled anywhere, because my parents didn't, and I was so ruled by a self-inflicted inferiority, that despite excelling in the top classes at school, I couldn't read a paragraph aloud without dying of fear.

I tell you all this because I could have stayed that way—insecure and contained—but God had something greater in store for me. God has something greater in store for all of us.

When a person experiences the Christian "rebirth" and becomes a believer, Jesus Christ enters her life and the seeds of greatness within are activated. What the born again, new believer then does with those seeds determines the rest of her life, and sets her up to either win or lose in life.

Keep It Simple

Now, thirty-five years after that encounter, I could share so many things. But let me highlight one thing in particular. I thank God that in the early years of my Christian experience, I discovered something that has proven to be very releasing—I simply learnt to keep things simple. When I became a Christian, I basically got saved and fell madly in love with Jesus Christ, the Son of God.

Did I plan to be a pastor's wife? No! Did I plan to be a pastor? No! (I didn't even know women could be pastors.) Did I plan to travel the world and meet awesome, world-changing people? No! Did I plan to find myself in a place of influence? No! Did I plan to marry one of this life's most wonderful men? Okay maybe! (Okay, okay, I am biased, but he is a great man of God, husband, father, provider and example, and I love him with all my heart.)

At fifteen, all of this would have terrified me, but what I distinctly planned to do was to love God and serve Him, whatever that meant. Trust me—within those seeds of greatness that I have been writing about lie the extraordinary and the exciting. However, God is very wise, and very rarely does He show us the full potential of the seed because He knows our frail human nature. He knows too well that some of us would faint, flee, or get a fat head. What I have discovered is that if we choose His way at each intersection of life, the seeds will deliver their full strength or their full potential. I also believe that if you keep certain things simple, the extraordinary and the exciting will definitely mark your life.

Keep *what* simple, you may ask?

Keep your heart simple. Keep it clean and uncluttered. Simply love God, and remain true to Him, others, and yourself. Brian has spent a lot of time unfolding the truth behind the scripture, "Keep your heart with all diligence, For out of it spring the issues of life" (Prov. 4:23). The word *issues* means "borders or parameters." Guard your heart diligently, and the borders or parameters of your little life just may expand further than you imagined.

Keep your desires simple. The psalmist wrote, "Delight yourself in the Lord and He will give you the desires of your heart" (Ps. 37:4 NIV). This portion of the Word is literally written on my heart. I discovered its gold when I was a young believer, and its reality has written itself all over my life, both spiritually and naturally. God has the remarkable ability to read our hearts and perceive our hidden imaginations, and grant them if He so desires. When you delight yourself in God, you ultimately end up delighting in what He delights in, and you find yourself constantly on the receiving end of His blessing.

Keep your relationships simple. Ensure that your relationships are clear, pure, and again, uncluttered. In Matthew 5:8, Jesus tells us that the pure in heart shall see God. When you encounter God, He has this remarkable ability to clean up your act, and when your act is cleaned up, it really affects the relationships in your life. When you keep your vertical relationship (God and you) clean, it positively affects your horizontal relationships (you and others).

Give People an Example to Follow

God wants you to be comfortable with who you are, but He also wants you to excel in life. The Word says, "Beloved, I pray that you may prosper in every way and [that your body] may keep well, even as [I know] your soul keeps well and prospers" (3 John 1:2 AMPLIFIED BIBLE).

Should you find yourself in a position of leadership with the responsibility of influence over others, then understand that you are commissioned and expected to excel. This is the beauty and price of leadership. Leadership is about giving people something to follow. Do not add unnecessary pressure or demand to this statement, because all you have to be is the person God calls you to be. If you achieve this, then you will find yourself fulfilling your part. As for me, I find myself married to a wonderful man of God, and together we find ourselves leaders of an incredible church and thousands of amazing people. I could add drama to my nervous system by putting unnecessary expectations upon myself, but what I have learned over the course of my journey is that I only have to be me. However, I do have certain responsibilities. I have to discover who I am, I must discover why I am on the planet, and then I must be sure to obey all that He asks me to do. I have a responsibility to give people a story worth following.

When the earthly lights fade and eternity dawns, and we find ourselves faced with a Day of Accountability, the very thing Christ

Jesus is going to inquire about is our calling (2 Tim. 1:9; Matt. 22:14). I dread to think how many will stand and say, "But Lord I was busy doing this and that . . ." and Christ may say "Yes, my love, but I didn't ask you to do this or that. I called you to do . . ."

Reproduce After Your Own Kind

In the church where I am planted, I am very aware that there are women who are more gifted and talented than me. Many of them are connecting with the awesome and divine call that is upon their lives, and my responsibility (as a leader in their lives) is to help them fulfill those calls. And if and when they soar higher and stronger than Bobbie Houston, fantastic! This sounds wonderful in theory, but it's amazing how many leaders can't exemplify this in reality. Instead of releasing and rejoicing, they feel threatened and redundant.

When I was newly saved, I received a prophetic word from a speaker at a youth camp. (Parents, encourage your kids to go to camp. God turns up and does wonderful things in our babies there.) The prophetic word said I would have "many, many children." Now when you are fifteen years old, "many, many children" can be a frightening concept (could that mean many, many stretch marks too?!). Well, of course God wasn't being literal—I have three beautiful children, and a few stretch marks to prove it, but the Lord was talking about spiritual children.

Often, I feel like an old mother hen. I look at the hundreds of incredible, stunning, beautiful, gorgeous (can you tell I love them?) young people in our congregation and I feel like a spiritual parent. What is the mark of a maternal heart? It is to love and to cherish, to protect and nurture, and to raise and release her off-spring to greater exploits than herself. You have spiritual children in your life, too! If every leader had this heart-attitude toward the people in their sphere of influence, the world would be a richer place. My husband calls it "a commitment to one another's prosperity." When you, especially as a leader, begin to express these unselfish qualities, you are beginning to truly carry the heartbeat of heaven.

To give and release, we must first discover and begin to fulfill our own purposes. Then inspiring others becomes the natural outcome. The challenge of handing the baton successfully to the next generation is in handing it in such a way that they connect easily, run faster, soar higher, and achieve more.

Time to Rise Up

We are living in truly exciting and significant times—days that God promised would be more awesome and glorious than at the beginning. Time to rise up! Time to get over the negatives. Time to get about your purpose. Time to get about being an inspiring example to all the people God has entrusted into your care, because believe me, they are watching. They are watching your behavior, your attitudes, your responses, and your relationships. They are watching your pattern of life! Paul tells us to "be an example [pattern] for the believers in speech, in conduct, in love, in faith, and in purity" (1 Tim, 4:12 AMPLIFIED BIBLE).

What pattern of living are you showing them? A good life? A happy life? A marriage that is growing stronger day by day? Great kids? Friendships that are sweet? If you are single, are you content in your singleness? Is whatever you put your hand to moving toward blessing and increase?

"I'll have what she's having!" Yes? No? Or absolutely!

I refer to the scene earlier in *When Harry Met Sally* when Sally fakes an orgasm. The word *orgasm* means "height, summit, zenith." Now forget the movie for the moment. Shouldn't we who are in Christ reach the summit, zenith, the utmost heights in life? I think so! Shouldn't we who are in God have the genuine experience? When it comes to life, let's not settle for a fake experience; let's go for the genuine article. There are so many things capable of containing this wonderful journey, so let's look at some of them and break the containment that limits so many.

PART 2

BREAK THE
CONTAINMENT

ent
INMENT

'Living with the restrictive parameters of 'I can't'
will not have you achieving your finest, and it
will not have you contributing to make the world
a better place.'

the containment

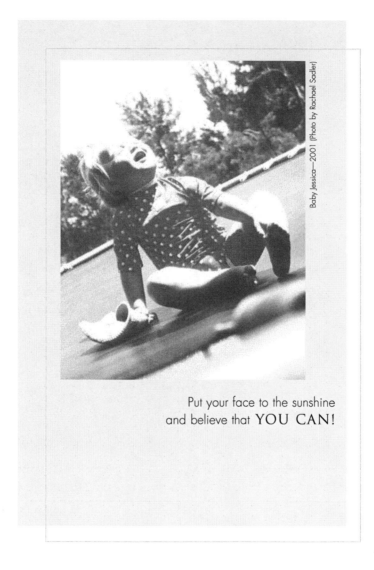

Baby Jessica—2001 (Photo by Rachael Sadler)

Put your face to the sunshine
and believe that YOU CAN!

CHAPTER FOUR

"I'm Inadequate"; "I Can't"; "I Have Nothing to Give"

Queen Victoria once said, "We are not interested in the possibilities of defeat." Defeat carries no victory and containment carries no victory. If my husband and I had allowed containment to triumph in our experience, there is a very good chance that neither of us would be doing what we are today, and Hillsong Church would not be having the influence and impact it is.

Our planet is filled with innumerable success stories. These stories belong to people who refused to be contained. They lifted the ceilings on their lives and discovered a universe of opportunity. For you to experience the same, you are going to have to deal with some fundamental challenges that are, in all honesty, common to all of us.

We all, at some time or another, can feel as if we are the only person on the entire planet going through a particular situation, but the reality is that there is nothing new under the sun.

Circumstances may differ, but humanity's challenges are common, which is why we can learn from one another's experiences. Heaven is very aware that life's lessons often come with a price tag. Proverbs 5:1 says, "Be attentive to my Wisdom [godly Wisdom learned by actual and costly experience]" (AMPLIFIED BIBLE). I smiled when I considered this thought. We are surrounded by thousands of great books written by great men and women of God. Their lives are often painstakingly and lovingly painted across the pages and we may read a paragraph and think, "Great point, I'll take note of that." The sobering reality is that the writer may have had to go to hell and back to come to that conclusion. They learned it by actual and costly experience, and it ends up being one paragraph in their books! The reader is the blessed one. If they take the truth offered and apply it, it may save them a trip to hell and back.

My heart is simply to share truth from my life and perspective. I often receive encouragement from other women in leadership and they will comment about my tendency to be open and transparent. Many have said how good it is to know that they are not alone. Transparency is wonderful as long as it produces answers. Transparency from a place of victory is a powerful tool. As life unfolds, we discover challenging issues are simply part of life's equation. Inability to address and overcome issues is what complicates life. I want to share a few things that had the capacity to contain my personal potential and also some specific challenges that attempted to contain our ministry.

"I'm Inadequate"

Ever spoken these words—"I'm inadequate! I'm so inadequate"?

If your beautiful little heart has ever cried these words, take courage; you are not the first and you certainly will not be the last to utter them. Truth be told, we are all inadequate. Inadequacy is not a major headache to God; however, *remaining inadequate* can definitely sabotage His master plan.

The dictionary defines *inadequate* as "insufficient." But rejoice and be encouraged because God's Word has definitely got this one covered. Sometimes we look at the lives of the Bible heroes and we think they must have been so cool, so amazing, so adequate in everything they attempted. *Wrong, wrong, wrong!* They were human, like us. They faced fear, insecurity, inferiority, and had their own feelings of personal inadequacy to deal with. Their individual stories often included neglect, lack, misunderstanding, and even abandonment. Their endeavors, which span the Bible's pages, are no more significant than ours today; it is just that God chose to position them early on in history, and made them prominent by recording them as examples.

We are also making history. We are fulfilling church history even today. Paul reminds us to be examples to our own generations (1 Tim. 4:12). We are to take the principles of God's unchanging Word and apply it to our own lives, so that we in turn may become living epistles (stories), "known and read by all men" (2 Cor. 3:2).

If you and I do not rise up and get in our appointed place at our appointed time, who will? The wicked and the unrighteous are certainly not going to bring the redemptive heart of God to a hurting planet. King David, despite his own sense of inadequacy, "served his own generation by the will of God" (Acts 13:36). We seriously need that same conviction if we are going to rescue the multitudes who are, every minute of every day, falling into a lost eternity.

Conviction is the quality that will help you rise above any inadequacy to achieve God's will and purpose in your life. Feeling inadequate? Let me encourage you with some stories from our beginnings. Brian and Bobbie Houston—hey, you're talking with the King and Queen of Inadequacy!

Today, Brian is a great communicator and leader, but it wasn't always that way. The first time he ever had to take devotions at Bible College, he felt so confident and felt like such a leader and such a man of God that he jumped in his car, drove in the opposite direction and conveniently "went missing"! When we started out in the ministry, I can remember being in a country town several hours drive from Sydney. I was eight and a half months pregnant (but looked about twelve months pregnant) and was asked to give a simple testimony. Heaven knows why I was there because I should have been nestled at home waiting for the impending birth of my ten-pound child. Anyway I gave it (the testimony, not the baby), sat down, pulled my waist-length, dark hair over my face and cried my eyes out because I felt so inadequate.

On another occasion, I can remember a television interview in the early years of a TV program hosted by fellow ministers in Sydney. I was terrified as we all sat there on those nice little couches waiting (waiting, waiting, waiting) to start. Then our host asked me this really simple question, "So Bobbie, what do you think of Brian?" I remember thinking, *Okay . . . I can do this! What do I think of Brian? . . . What do I think of Brian . . . uh huh . . . um . . . How hard is this, Bobbie? What do I think of Brian?* Total blanks-ville!

Do I need to go on? Are you starting to feel better? Inadequate? Girl, you are not alone. Remember that being inadequate is not a problem to God. God is a *nothing* expert! He loves to mold awesome things out of what seems like nothing. The problem is when we *choose* to remain inadequate.

"I Can't"

Allow me to be strong here. Living within the restrictive parameters of "I can't" will not have you achieving your finest, and it will certainly not have you contributing to make the world a better place. We live in a world where the enemy's destructive forces are rapidly advancing. All of us need to quit saying "I can't" and all of us need to start saying "I *can!*" Our willingness to step out beyond our fear, insecurity, and inadequacy just might bring urgently needed light and life to someone's painful existence.

I frequently succumbed to this thinking when we were starting out in ministry because I felt so inadequate and incapable of what seemed a huge calling and requirement. When Brian and I first began to travel and minister, the first thing people would often ask me was, "Oh, you're the pastor's wife, how sweet. What do you do, dear? Do you sing, play the piano perhaps?"

I am sure their intentions were innocent, but when you are twenty-two years old, negotiating a brand new baby, have just driven eight to ten hours in the stifling Australian outback heat with no air conditioning (squashed between bassinette and PA gear), have no money, feel out of your depth, and are totally insecure, this is not what you need to hear. *No, I don't do anything. I don't sing, I don't play piano (remember, my parents thought learning guitar was a phase and I would grow out of it), I'm useless, I can't do anything, I'm a failure.* Thank God that the church has grown up and matured, and that many of the misconceptions and expectations of what a pastor's wife should or should not do, have been replaced by more realistic expectations.

Our challenge is to grow beyond our inadequacies and in doing so, we will all feel less inclined to say "I can't." Let me be kind to you. We all feel inadequate until we start to grow! The reason I used to say this was, to a degree, because I couldn't. I was just starting out in the school of life and the school of the Spirit. How can you give away something that is not within you yet? How can you teach or impart something if you have never learned it yourself? Paul challenges us to devote ourselves to reading, teaching, and instilling the Word (1 Tim. 4:13). He continues in verse 15 to say that we should practice, cultivate and meditate upon these things.

Perhaps right now you can't do something, but you can begin to apply yourself to grow. We live in a world with incredible resources. God has destined this generation for greatness, and the resources, the tools, and the wisdom are readily available. All we have to do is look for them and then apply to our lives. If something becomes a priority in our lives, it is amazing how we can make it happen.

I have the wonderful privilege of teaching our Hillsong women on a regular basis. As a church we have a strong conviction about the value and potential of women. We are totally committed to developing and releasing them into the fullness of their destiny and calling. We have consistently taught them the reality that God seriously wants to use them. Consequently, many of these women have availed themselves of our various training and college courses, and are preparing themselves for what they believe their futures hold.

I remember on one occasion asking this same company of women a question: "Stand up if you believe that in the days that are ahead, you will preach and declare the things of God?" They all stood up. I said, "No, you didn't understand. Sit down. Now, stand up if you believe that, in the days that are ahead, you will preach and declare the things of God?" They all stood up again! I thought, *Okay God, I guess this is the principle of reproducing after your own kind.* I then proceeded to passionately pray for them.

"I can't" can also indicate a lack of faith. In reality, those terrible little words are saying, "God, You can't." That statement puts you in disagreement with Him because His Word says, "I can do all things through Christ who strengthens me" (Phil. 4:13), "all things are possible" (Matt. 19:26 NIV), and "my power (ability) is made perfect in weakness (inability)" (2 Cor. 12:9 NIV, commentary mine). Everything in God's Word tells us that *we can!*

"I Have Nothing to Give"

Have you ever been asked to do something and then found yourself saying or thinking, "Oh, I'd love to help, but I do not know what to do," or "Oh, I want to, but what will I say?" or "Sorry, I can't help, I feel like I've got nothing to give." If you feel like you have nothing to give or contribute, it may be that you have sown a famine instead of a harvest in your own life.

Since the day I met Christ, I have never ceased to love Him, and for me to walk away from Him is an absolutely abhorrent thought (shudder, shudder). However, there was a period in my life when life was very hectic (what's changed?) and when I think I neglected to grow spiritually. How did this happen? To be brutally honest, I think I slipped into a spiritual hole for a season when I first had my children. I never missed a service but somehow seemed to miss the sermons. Pacifying young children can often remove you from the sound of the Word, which is designed to be our lifeline. I think most proactive churches these days provide great parent rooms with TV monitors, and most churches who place a healthy emphasis on teaching make sure that such women (or men) have access to recorded teaching resources.

I think I also failed to grow in personal Bible reading because I would leave my reading until the last thing at night and would (you guessed it) fall asleep three or four verses in. The Word wasn't boring—I've always loved God's Word—rather it was because this young mum was exhausted. Does this sound familiar to any of you? At that time, I also failed to read books, because I couldn't or I didn't know how to make time to read. Consequently, this busy young mum sowed a famine in her own life. I didn't mean to, I just did. Had I honestly realized what I was neglecting, I am sure I would have done something about it.

So dear friend, if you are sowing a famine in your life, do not be surprised if you feel inadequate. When I realized this, I chose to change. God didn't punish me, instead He promised to restore to me the lost opportunity. I love my God; He is just so loving and kind!

Many people (even leaders) fail to position themselves for growth and consequently feel they have nothing substantial to give. As Christians, if we are not growing, we are stagnating. In fact, growth is such a critical aspect of our destinies that we must learn to confront and overcome any challenges in our lives that would hinder our growth. We need to continually and aggressively confront containment.

CHAPTER FIVE

Confront the Containment

Our responsibility is to discern what is happening in our own lives, and then actively position ourselves so we can address the issues that are potentially detrimental. Paul wrote, "Therefore my dear ones . . . work out [cultivate, carry out to the goal, and fully complete] your own salvation with reverence and awe and trembling" (Phil. 2:12 AMPLIFIED BIBLE). Too often Christians want God to do the hard yards for them, but this is not what we read in these verses. God expects us to actively and diligently pursue our destiny goal. Thankfully He doesn't leave us to our own devices because, as Paul continued to say, "[Not in your own strength] for it is God Who is all the while effectively at work in you [energizing and creating in you the power and desire], both to will and to work for His good pleasure and satisfaction and delight" (v 13). That's reassuring, isn't it? I'd hate to have to do this thing called life without His strength.

Position Yourself by Reading God's Word

Many Christians fail to read God's Word regularly and then wonder why their lives aren't enlarging as they should. Satan, our adversary who desires to steal our potential, will do anything to prevent you from getting into the Word. As we enter glorious and challenging days for the church, the Christians who will be easy targets for the enemy will be the ones who fail to allow God's Word to become grafted into their hearts and lives. The word *graft* is likened to a strong vine twisting itself around you. When the Word of God is entwined in and through your life, nothing can prevail against you because nothing can prevail against the living Word. No storm or adversity can blow you off course, and no demon from the pit of hell can knock you down. The Word of God has the power to change, renew, equip, and enable you. Perhaps you do not like the way you are. Okay, the Word is not just a concept to change you; it has the power to change you. If you want to change, then seriously get into the Word and you will.

Perhaps you need renewing. You do not like being bound to the old. Well, the Word promises to renew. Everything in life is deteriorating but the Word has the supernatural ability to take you in the opposite direction. It can renew your life, energy, spontaneity and the big life God intended for you. Perhaps you need equipping. Then the Word will place in your hand what is needed. It will put movement in your legs, words in your mouth, compassion in your heart, and tools in your hand. (How awesome!) Perhaps you need enabling. We actually cannot do much by ourselves. What we need to do is partner with the Spirit of God and the Word of God. We need to follow the Spirit's lead. Ephesians 6:17 it says of the wonderful Holy Spirit, "take the Sword that the Spirit wields, which is the Word of God" (AMPLIFIED BIBLE).

I promise, you will no longer feel inadequate when the Word is rich within you. You must make it a priority, just as putting food in your mouth is a priority (and heaven knows, that is definitely not a problem for some of us!) Second Timothy 3:16 - 17 reveals how equipping the Word is: "Every Scripture is God-breathed [given by His inspiration] and profitable for instruction, for reproof and conviction of sin, for correction of error and discipline in obedience, [and] for training in righteousness [in holy living, in conformity to God's will in thought, purpose, and action], so that the man of God may be complete and proficient, well-fitted and thoroughly equipped for every good work" (AMPLIFIED BIBLE).

Okay, now go back and read that verse again. This time meditate on what God is saying. For example, just meditate for a second on the fact that "every scripture is God-breathed." God-breathed. What you are reading from Scripture has the breath of Almighty God, Creator of the Universe on it. It carries life; it is awesome and amazing! I am inspired, how about you? Words such as "I'm inadequate," "I can't," and "I have got nothing to give" soon begin to disappear as God's Word enriches you.

Position Yourself in the House of God

Do not just attend church, be the church! Do not be one of those weak Christians who looks for excuses to avoid the house of God. God ordained the church with powerful dynamics that will establish growth and blessing in your life. Ephesians 4:16 says that when all the limbs and ligaments get to know each other, start liking each other, and start working in unity, then the body becomes healthy and happy. Expansion is the natural by-product.

The church of Jesus Christ is not a building. It is a powerful company of believers who constitute the bride of Christ. Christ loves His bride. He is crazy about her. He laid His life down for her, and she is the only thing He said He would build. Wisdom would tell me that if the church is this important to God Almighty, it ought to be a priority to me also. God also likens His church to a family. Healthy families are relational—they actually like each other and lovingly support one another when need arises. Imagine a brilliant family, full of life and energy, buzzing with kids and adults and all their respective friends. Plenty of food, plenty of noise and mess, and basically nobody wanting to go to bed, because it's so exciting they might miss something. Now you've got a glimpse of what God's church should look like.

I love my church. Hillsong Church is very much a family. It is full of life and enthusiasm and I gauge its health by the fact that our people are "church-a-holics"—they cannot get enough of the place! In my book *Heaven Is in This House*, I give greater expression to all I believe the house of God can bring to the world we inhabit. Get into church life and contribute something! Even if it seems really small and insignificant to you, contribute it. I guarantee that our amazing God who sees everything will pour back into you. Now here's the groovy part. He is a God of increase therefore He will always give back with increase, therein enlarging your capacity and world. As your life enlarges, feeling inadequate will soon become a thing of the past.

For this reason Paul advises Christians, "Forsake not to gather together, as is the custom of some" (Heb. 10:25 NLT). The Word also teaches that many are sick and weak because they are not truly a part of the Lord's Body. Many people limit this portion of Scripture to communion only, but He was also passionately talking about church life, church attendance and the dynamic that is the house of God. Many Christians want to flourish in life, but not on God's terms. The Word declares that those who truly flourish are those that are planted in the house of God (Ps. 92:13).

Position Yourself to Learn from Others

Over the years, my home and car have accumulated an array of books and teaching CDs. There are countless godly men and women in this race from whom we can learn. Start reading good, God-honoring, faith-building, inspiring books, and start listening to great teachers who will help your faith increase. Some people might say, "I can't afford it" or "I can't find the time." But you actually cannot afford not to. Prioritize your time and finances to invest in your own life. And if there are those in your world who might be struggling financially, why not start a lending library, so once you are done with a teaching resource or book, you can help bless someone else's life with it? Secular magazines and television may or may not harm you, but they do not necessarily nourish your soul. Women's cars are frequently called "mum's taxi," so why shouldn't all that time you spend in the car running your kids here, there, and everywhere be profitable? Instead of whining because you haven't had a life of your own since your kids became mobile, you could actually be learning something.

Look into how you can budget your finances so that you can attend some of the great conferences that are available these days. There are certain churches in all the continents of the world that are commissioned and anointed by God to host great conferences. These people are prepared to carry enormous budgets and work hard to bring some of the finest teachers to your land. Find out what is happening and take advantage of the resource that God is providing.

If you are a minister and leader, it could be considered conceited and selfish to think you know it all and do not need to read, observe and learn from others. You owe it to your congregation or those in your sphere of influence (not to mention yourself) to grow. I admire my husband, who although a leader in his field in our nation, always makes sure he has people in his life who can challenge him to greater heights. We love and value friends that the Lord has brought into our lives at various times who have helped enlarge our understanding regarding faith, generosity, and so much more. In turn, as we have appropriated these truths into our lives, it has flowed from us to others and proven a blessing. "As iron sharpens iron, so a man sharpens the countenance of his friend" (Prov. 27:17). Our friends have sharpened our ministry and I know we have been a blessing to them as well.

Brian and I are in relationship with many leaders, yet it never ceases to amaze us that many times the pastors and leaders who struggle the most or feel isolated and alone fail to come to the very things that will either encourage them or stretch them into new levels of release. None of us graduate from the school of learning. These are strong words, I know, but true nonetheless for many, and we all need to realize that the stretching and growing always preempts enlargement and blessing. Friends, we need each other. *We need each other.* Position yourself among people who can impart into you. And remember, as you grow, God will take the fruit of your growth and plant it in others. Herein lies the principle of multiplication.

I sometimes joke with our young people, telling them, "You have no excuse for not achieving your finest potential because you sit under great teaching. Any wisdom we have, we have freely given to you, and we continue to expose you to the finest teachers from around the world." But then, like many things in life, choice is up to the individual. God gave Jesus to the world in order that we may know and enjoy good success (Jer. 29:11), yet so many still choose to ignore Him. A person can be exposed to all the knowledge and understanding in the universe, but if they do not take it and apply it personally, it will never become wisdom in their own experience.

The Word says that you "shall know the truth and the truth shall set you free" (John 8:32 DARBY). Hearing the truth isn't enough; being familiar with the truth isn't enough; having the truth on your bedside table isn't enough. You have to take it, read it and apply it to your heart. It is then that you are set free.

Wisdom is applied knowledge that makes you skillful in living life to its fullest. Proverbs 4:8 says that if you prize wisdom, she will bring good success into your life, and James 4:5 says that if we lack wisdom, we must simply pray and ask God for it. So often heaven is poised, ready to help us, and we simply and sadly forget to ask.

Our goal should be to have stories of powerful testimony, where a woman may look at another woman who is skillful in managing a home, a marriage, a business, or whatever, and ponder, "How does she do it?" In her heart she may silently say, "I want what she's got." Then one day (somewhere in this equation of friendship), the pondering one will actually ask, "What makes you tick? I want what you've got."

Position Yourself to Grow in Faith

The Word talks often of being responsible with the measure of talent, gift, or faith we have been given. We need to learn to use and grow what we have been given. I once woke up and thought, "I need more faith." I felt like the Holy Spirit spoke straight back and said, "Well, apply the measure in your hand and We'll give you more." (Doesn't that sound just like a parent?) That measure can apply to many areas in life. The first year in a marriage, a newborn child, or an initial response of obedience in a pioneering work are all measures. Handle them carefully, faithfully, and wisely, and they will blossom into something magnificent.

The Father desires us to have the same conviction as Moses and those whose testimonies are summarized in Hebrews 11. They were a company of men and women who chose to grow in faith. They successfully negated all that would hinder their potential. Listen to the awesome voices of their testimonies from the Amplified Bible's Hebrews 11:

- "For by [faith—trust and holy fervor born of faith] the men of old had divine testimony borne to them and obtained a good report . . . "(v 2) *Could that mean that women-of-old could have had other women-of-old looking at them, thinking, "I'll have what she's having"?*

- "[Prompted, actuated] by faith Abel brought a better and more acceptable sacrifice . . ." (v 4) *Is there something within you that deeply desires to please God? Growing in faith will do it.*

- "Because of faith Enoch was caught up and transferred into heaven . . ." (v 5) *Now there is a crazy thought!*

- "[Prompted] by faith Noah, being forewarned by God concerning events of which as yet there was no visible sign, took heed and diligently and reverently constructed and prepared an ark for the deliverance of his own family (v 7). *Hey, here's a concept. Could we possibly rescue the human race? We have many business people in our church whose goal is to fund the Salvation of the Earth. Grandiose? Extreme? But prompted, activated, and resourced by faith, they just may succeed and contribute powerfully to God's will on the earth.*

- "[Urged on] by faith Abraham, when he was called, obeyed and went forth . . . . [Prompted] by faith he dwelt as a temporary resident in the land which was designated . . ." (v 8–9) *Heard someone once say once that two-thirds of God's name is go. Oh no, not strange, scary places. I cannot possibly go to strange, scary places . . . sound familiar?*

- "Because of faith Sarah herself received . . ." (v 11) *Got any promises you are still waiting to receive?*

- "By faith Abraham, when he was put to the test . . . " (v 17) *Do not get nervous now, faith always has its test.*

- "[With eyes of] faith Isaac, looking far into the future . . ." (v 20) *Hey, do you think he might have seen us?*

- "[Prompted] by faith Jacob, when he was dying, blessed . . ." (v 21) *We are stewards over future generations. Bless them by being a woman or person of faith.*

- "[Actuated] by faith Joseph . . . referred to [the promise of God] . . . " (v 22) *Now excuse me, Lord . . . remember that promise!*

- "[Prompted] by faith Moses . . . became great . . ." (vv 23–24) *God has expended a lot of energy over the centuries trying to make us understand that seeds of greatness are within us all. Wise up babe!*

- "By faith (simple trust and confidence in God) [Moses] instituted and carried out the Passover and the sprinkling of the blood [on the door post], so that the destroyer of the firstborn [the angel] might not touch those [of the children of Israel]" (v 28).

Those of us in leadership have been commissioned, alongside the men, to rise in faith and lead the church successfully into her future. How do we do this? How do we grow in faith? There are countless answers to that question, but I think the simplest formula is found in Romans 10:17: "So faith comes by hearing, and hearing by the Word of Christ" (NASB). Simply read and respond to your Bible, and simply listen and respond when the Word is brought to you in the house where you are planted. This will produce faith in your heart, which supernaturally enables you to access His bountiful grace, which then empowers you in life and ministry. Discovering this will negate all the things that would hinder, prevent, or contain you.

Photo by Femia Shirliff

Gorgeous Donna telling it like it is

{ COLOUR 2001 }

CHAPTER SIX

Mindsets, Enemies, and Spiritual Blindness

Mindsets are more powerful than most people realize. They have the capacity to distort reality and ultimately sabotage potential. Perspective that is framed or determined by truth is essential if you are going to live a life of impact and influence. Too many women (and men for that matter) shortchange themselves in life because they lose sight of the big picture.

The Big Picture

Problems so often arise when we lose sight of *why* we are doing something. It is then very easy to lose that perspective I've been talking about and feel victimized, so it is imperative that you never take your eyes off the big picture, or the finish line of life. Any woman who has given birth will relate to this analogy. You'll agree that to enjoy the miracle of a newborn baby, you have to travel the nine months of stretching and growing, and the inevitable moment of birth cannot be escaped. I remember just before I delivered our third child Laura (9 pounds, 12 ounces, 23½ inches long, and she was not my largest) I felt this strange need for help! I remember very sweetly asking the nurse, who had just come on duty, for something for the pain. She, fresh from a good night's sleep and in her size 0 uniform, looked at me and said, "Let's see if we can go a little longer, shall we?" Of course I smiled (I always smile, I'm basically a nice person), but inside I was screaming, *Excuse me. Excuse me! How dare you say let's see if we can just go a little longer?! What do you know?! What do you mean we? You've just come on duty; I've been here nine months!*

When you lose sight of the big picture (in my case, the beautiful baby to come), the negatives and challenges of that journey crowd in and make us a little crazy. The negatives even have the potential to sell us a lie! Sadly, I have encountered women who are married to leaders that feel as if the call is their enemy, or to put it more bluntly, they feel like the church has become their enemy. This incorrect perception grows in their minds and before they know it, they are believing a bunch of untruths. My desire is to help such women better understand the conviction that has them traveling the path they are on.

Partnership Is a Healthy Mindset

Marriage is a partnership, and the Word clearly teaches that no house divided stand. I have observed that men who fail to include their wives in their lives or destiny paths are asking for trouble, and women who refuse to be involved or fail to understand are also asking for trouble. It happens in the secular arena, and sadly it happens in Christian ministry as well. Your participation in that partnership can be expressed in many ways. You may be actively involved and your presence may be felt, or you may be the quiet supporter, but in your heart of hearts, you must establish that you are united and running the race of life together.

In the early seasons of our ministry, the Lord gave me a real understanding of this partnership. I loved serving God with Brian, but as I have said, I felt inadequate and didn't know where or how I fitted into the picture. So God being the gracious Father that He is, spoke very clearly to me and whispered "Sweetheart, Brian's fruit is your fruit as well." (I don't know how God communicates with you, but I often feel Him use words like this to me.) That still, small, and calming voice on an altar call many years ago released me. It freed my spirit, established a good stronghold in my mind, and allowed me the space to grow out of my insecurity and inadequacy. It literally allowed me to release my husband to extensive travel, it allowed me to understand the long hours that are often involved in building anything substantial and lasting, and it gave God room to teach me how to handle and negotiate the challenges of life in the fast lane.

This predominantly became my life attitude or life mindset and has, in turn, positively affected our children. We live a fast, demanding, and exciting life committed to establishing God's kingdom here on earth. Our children, who are now all young adults, do not see the pace and demands of that calling as an enemy to their lives, but are instead equally committed. And I might add, are equally blessed and favored by that very same attitude.

Young women sometimes ask me, "How do you prioritize;

how do you juggle it all?" Of course we need wisdom, and there are times when I have certainly bitten off a little more than I could successfully chew, but it's to no advantage to resent those times. Life is a learning process, so try to view such experiences as learning curves. What is imperative, however, is that all the things that we become involved in are necessary in relation to the plan God has for our lives. Each one of us will have an opinion regarding priorities and I respect that. However in our world, we often refuse to legislate the order. What really matters is that nothing really important is being neglected. We have countless friends and colleagues whose winning experience proves you can have it all. A little God-wisdom, a little sensitivity, some clever planning, respect for the seasonal ebb and flow of life, and a sense of determination has them enjoying God, church, passion, kids, family, friends, and others. The cat and the dog get fed, the in-laws are happy, and hopefully the garden is a good testimony.

I have to be honest here and say that sometimes we can all fall victim to the old tell-tale dark circles under the eyes. We can even succumb to irritability if we so choose, but that's only because our bodies are mortal. The spirit is truly alive and well and having a ball in life, but the old body needs an early night every now and then. The only thing that we are religious about is having our day off on Mondays. If we are in town, then we guard this day. It is imperative to rest and pace yourself (and catch up on domestic activities) if you intend to finish your course well.

As believers, let's never take on poor attitudes regarding hard work and diligence. As people called to be examples of a higher standard, let's exemplify a work ethic that astounds the unredeemed world. The secular arena correctly applauds hard work and success but tends not to understand the same dynamics within the church or kingdom of God. Hillsong Church is a strong ministry because, since its inception, we have consistently applied biblical principles of hard work, selflessness, and generosity. Some onlookers may have their opinions regarding this, but the reality is that God's principles work, enabling us as a ministry to be more effective in helping people. The gospel message may be free, but taking this gospel message to a lost world takes hard work and a lot of finance.

Reward Is a God-Concept

Never allow faulty mindsets to limit your potential for reward. Love what you do and be faithful, because faithful hearts are always rewarded. In the early years of our marriage, Brian began to travel overseas. I wasn't able to go with him because our finances and young family didn't allow it. I could easily have developed resentment. I remember when he and three other friends ventured to England for the very first time. They couldn't conceal their excitement. At the airport I kept a stiff upper lip (very British in retrospect), trying so desperately to be happy for them. As they disappeared through the departure gate, tears rolled down my face and continued to roll down my face for three days. On the way home from the airport I even stopped to do my most favorite thing (window shop at my favorite furniture store) in the hope that it would snap me out of my sudden misery. Our son Joel was a toddler and kept saying from the back seat of the car, "What's wrong, mummy? What's wrong?"

I think my heartache was simply that it felt as if there was no consolation prize for being the faithful releasing wife. I was truly happy for Brian and our friends to go on their exciting adventure, but I felt left behind again. At 3 a.m. on the third night, I sat up in bed and cried , "God, this is ridiculous! I cannot cry for the entire four weeks. Please help me!" I will never exchange that experience, because that night my Savior came in our bedroom and I felt Heaven whisper, "Child, your reward is with Me." You see dear friend, if you remain faithful and if you refuse to see the call as an enemy to your life, God will honor and reward you.

Many years ago, I sowed tears when it came to travel, and now all these years later, I find myself truly reaping. Every time I board a plane, I thank God for the awesome privilege of experiencing this amazing planet and her people. In addition, our children are also blessed. It is amazing how you can bless your kids (and others) on accumulated frequent flyer points! Remember what the Amplified Bible says about being "blessed, happy, fortunate and to be envied" (Gen. 30:13). One thing I will add here about my children is that they seldom, if ever, complained. They have always lovingly released their parents to the greater mandate, and I believe this attitude has brought reward to them. They were blessed children, who have now grown into blessed young adults, who in turn are making their own personal impact on the world.

Patience Is a Friend

Patience is not a consolation prize. It is a powerful partner to faith. Patience is the ability to stand strong on the Word and His promises when your reward or victory is slow in coming. It is the force that will secure the promises of God in your life, causing you to end up perfect, complete and wanting for nothing! God is never slow—His timing is actually perfect, and if you have walked any distance with Him, you will know this to be true.

James wrote, "But let endurance and steadfastness and patience have full play and do a thorough work, so that you may be [people] perfectly and fully developed [with no defects], lacking in nothing" (James 1:4 AMPLIFIED BIBLE). Whatever your story, friend, connect with what you are called to achieve. Life is too short to be involved in what doesn't have eternal value, and life is too short to fight unnecessary battles.

Real Enemies to Contend With

Life can be defined as a journey or pilgrimage. Its course is lined with opportunity and adventure, and if you apply wisdom, your story will unfold beautifully. However, the journey is marked with real challenges and real enemies. They are not figments of the imagination of Hollywood screenwriters. They are very real and if allowed, they have the capacity to divert you from your destiny. When the children of Israel were heading towards the Promised Land, they failed to successfully negotiate a few bends and curves, failed to recognize challenges that God intended them to overcome, and failed to deal properly with certain giants. All in all, they made what was meant to be a very fast journey into a very long journey, and then eventually died before they arrived. (How tragic was that?) I sometimes wonder, did it ever occur to them that perhaps God wanted them to get where they were going in His perfect timing because He had things for them to accomplish? It is imperative, therefore, that we intelligently recognize the dynamics of our individual journeys.

Allow Each Season Its Designed Purpose

God desires that we negotiate our courses in the correct time frames. Seasons have their allocated times and purposes, and will inevitably dovetail with one another. New seasons may merge gently into your experience, or they may arrive abruptly on your doorstep. The key is in recognizing the season, and having the capacity to allow each season its purpose. Therefore, do not camp longer than you are supposed to, do not resent one season over another, do not confuse seasons, and definitely do not try to skip a season either. Too often people try or expect to reap where they have never sown. Decide to intelligently meet the challenges of each season.

Don't Camp Longer Than You Are Supposed To

Have you ever met believers who tediously run around the same old mountain year after year? Patience and endurance is one thing, but life is way too short (and precious) to get stuck in a rut. In Psalm 23:4, David exclaimed, "Even though I walk through the valley of the shadow of death, I will fear no evil" (NIV). Notice he was walking *through* the valley. Do not camp there! Keep those legs moving. Your Christian growth and experience should be continual, always moving onwards and upwards. Obviously "walking through" may take a period of time. You may have to pitch your tent and figuratively stay overnight, but do not live there. Do not change your address to Valley of the Shadow of Death!

Often a valley is simply the experience between one mountain and the next higher mountain. God is continuously calling us higher and higher, because victory is secured as we ascend with Him, however, to experience each new "mountain-top experience," we have to negotiate what lies in between. God wants us to walk with a victory attitude that has us rejoicing and authoritative, no matter what the terrain looks like. That's why David could sing like he did in the midst of the shadow of Death.

Don't Resent One Season Over Another

Learn to appreciate and value each season. Each season has a divine purpose. That is not to say that God allows tragic events to happen to us. He doesn't. God is a good God and only good things flow from His hand. Romans 8:28 says that all things work together for good, to those that love God (and do not drop their bundle!) This means that God in His sovereignty is able to cause a disastrous situation to turn around as we appropriate His wisdom and grace.

I remember teaching our women about the amazing qualities of the soldier, the athlete, and the farmer as referred to in 2 Timothy 2. So easily we can approach a new horizon, a new season, or a new level in life and carry a certain expectation. Perhaps we imagine major reward, major profit, or major vacation. We are expecting growth, expansion, or a luxury holiday in Hawaii, and our beautiful heavenly Father says, "Sorry darling, there are still some battles to be won" (so put your bikini away and keep your army fatigues on); or "Sorry sweetheart, there is still hard ground to be turned" (so do not put your plough down yet); or "Sorry my love, there is still a stretch of road to run" (so tighten the laces on your running shoes).

Allow me to share from my world. The first substantial spiritual battle that Hillsong Church faced was prior to the construction on our facilities. As a church, we had spent many years gathering resources and it was a very special day when we actually put the first spade in the ground. When a church puts a natural stake in the ground, it is like putting a spiritual stake in the head of the enemy. The devil is working overtime because this earth, which he mistakenly thinks is his domain, is rapidly being reclaimed by a victorious and advancing church. During that period of construction, we faced a challenging season, but in retrospect, do we resent that season? Of course not! It was actually fantastic because we learned firsthand about endurance, diligence, spiritual warfare, God's favor, and much more. We decided not to resent the process, but rather glean all the lessons, gold and victory we could.

Don't Confuse Seasons

The enemy would love to confuse the issues at hand. He would love to have us relaxing on the porch drinking coffee when we should be sowing seed. He would love to sidetrack us into complacency when we should be taking a deep breath because the home stretch has come into view. He would love to have us fighting in the barracks when the source of contention is actually coming from the outside. Remember King David? He was supposed to be at war, but instead he found himself wandering around on a rooftop and falling prey to mischief. Ask God to give you wisdom so you can discern what each season is supposed to be teaching you.

Don't Try to Skip a Season

Every season is vital to the journey, and trying to skip a season just doesn't work. Imagine your life as a scale. It will have a starting point and a finishing point. Now think about this with me. Every single piece of that scale is important. Not one season or stage on that timescale is insignificant. It is not supposed to be a dotted line with big gaps (unless of course, you like living in or falling into black holes!).

Here's a little exercise designed to bring perspective to your journey: Stop and consider your life thus far. Ask yourself, "What was achieved, what did I learn in all these various stages of my life?" Here is a brief outline of some key moments in my own personal timescale to help you better understand this point:

- **Age 0–14**: A secure and strong foundation of love is laid, despite a non-church upbringing.
- **Age 15–19**: My first church experience in New Zealand. Excellent teaching and Christian foundation laid. Principles of faithfulness begin to be tested in my life.
- **Age 19–21**: The second church where I experienced my season of courtship, engagement, and marriage. Wonderful.
- **Age 21–27**: Moved to Sydney. A very exciting season of six years serving the leadership and vision of Brian's father.

Proving-ground, I think, of my willingness to give God
my all.

- **Age 27– 42:** Planted the Hills campus of Hillsong Church.
Pioneer spirit exercised, and maturity and development of
both the natural and spiritual.

- **Age 42 and Onwards:** Another stretch as our world
expanded to embrace the leadership of the City campus of
Hillsong, and all the endeavors that recent years have
brought.

I value and appreciate all of these stages, and realize that
each of them prepared and literally opened the door for the next
season.

Open Your Eyes and Face the Future Straight On

Life, marriage, raising future generations, building dreams,
and securing success are some of the wonderful seasons we get to
experience and enjoy. Wisdom tells us to open our eyes to this big
wonderful life. The enemy would love to inhibit our effectiveness
by keeping us blind and ignorant to what is happening around us.
Soldiers, athletes, and farmers who walk around with their eyes
closed are not very effective. The Bible tells us that, "the god of
this world has blinded the unbelievers' minds [that they should
not discern the truth], preventing them from seeing the illuminating light of the Gospel of the glory of Christ [the Messiah],
Who is the Image and Likeness of God" (2 Cor. 4:4 AMPLIFIED
BIBLE). God is not trying to keep any of us in darkness. Unbelievers
are blind, because the enemy, Satan, keeps them in darkness. So

we have to pray the "spiritual blinders" off them, so that they might see the Light and choose Jesus.

However, believers can sometimes allow their visions to become a little blurred. It is almost like they walk around squinting. Imagine a Christian walking around squinting with their nose pulled up. How attractive is that? From my perspective, I do not think that looks like the authoritative-Lion-of-Judah-kind of Christian who is going to accomplish great things on the earth. Certainly that picture validates unbelievers saying, "I'm definitely *not* having what that person is having." God would much prefer us wide-eyed, alert, and knowing exactly where we are going in life.

Do not allow anything to distract or divert you, even the tiniest of things. Throughout the ages, the devil and his cohorts have not increased in number, but they have become very clever at what they do. His deceptions are the same, so it's important to see things from God's perspective. If we do not, unimportant things become wrongly magnified, important things lose focus, and direction becomes confused. So eyes wide open, my friend. Clear away the spiritual sleepy-dust, and let's learn to live in the ever-increasing illuminating light of the gospel. It will help you negotiate life with success and ease.

In the next section of this book, I want to share about being focused, determined, and unshakable. There is nothing sweeter on the planet than a beautiful woman who is succeeding in negotiating the curves and bends of life. After all, it is your journey—so it is up to you to negotiate it well.

PART 3

NEGOTIATE YOUR
JOURNEY WELL

'The object of the **Journey**—
to arrive unscathed and with everyone you left home with'

negotiate

\jour'ney\, n.
1. an act of going from one place to another
2. travel or passage from one place to another;
   hence figuratively, a passage through life

JOURNEY

journey

your journey well

Take up the challenges
TOGETHER

CHAPTER SEVEN

Recognize the Challenge

Arriving at your pre-determined destination unscathed and with everyone you left home with is the objective of the journey. I wonder if the Host of Heaven and the angels ever stand poised on the edge of heaven, mouths gasping, hair on end, hands in the air, watching our antics down here on earth? I sometimes wonder if, for example, the apostle Paul doesn't get frustrated with us. He endured so much pain himself in order to save us pain, and yet we often do not avail ourselves of this wisdom. As individuals, we obviously want to arrive at our destination and receive our rewards, but as responsible leaders, we also want to arrive with everyone who has been entrusted into our care.

When I stand one day before my Creator, I want to stand before Him with my husband, my kids, and the entire congregation of Hillsong Church. I do not want one single person to be missing. There will be thousands of us, and judging by the way we carry on down here, it'll be a very loud, noisy, fantastic moment of uncontained excitement!

Understand the Process

If we do not learn to negotiate our own personal journeys, we will sabotage the moment, not only for ourselves, but for others. There is a process for every individual and it is up to us to be intelligent about our own lives. Every journey carries specific challenges, and then occasionally specific enemies can come against us as well.

For example, if you are a woman who has chosen a professional career, you will recognize and agree that long hours of committed study come with the process of choosing such a path. Decide to be a doctor, lawyer, or teacher and it is wasted energy resenting or trying to escape the process that involves an intense season (sometimes years) of study. Many people want the reward of progress, but without the process. They are not prepared to pay the price of the journey.

Perhaps you are a woman gifted in the arts. You will recognize that many years of diligence go into developing and perfecting a gift in music, dance, or drama. Our church is blessed with many wonderful singers and musicians, and a definite aspect of our influence as a church is in the area of worship. All who minister on our platform recognize that their ministries involve a process of rehearsals, early starts, and diligence in bringing their God-given gifts to a place of God-honoring excellence. They realize it would be wasted energy to resent or try to escape the requirement of being at rehearsals two hours before everyone else. Why? Because it is simply the process of answering the call on their lives.

Perhaps your life's journey has dealt you an unexpected circumstance or two. I have a dear friend who has been entrusted with a special and unique calling—she has a beautiful daughter confined to a wheelchair. We all believe in faith that one day Victoria will run and play and express her energy like other young people. But in the meantime, does my friend resent or try to escape the process of this circumstance? Of course not. She strengthens her arms (literally) for the journey (process) she finds herself traveling.

Being in Christian ministry, there are specific things that are unique to my journey. Men and women involved in such leadership carry the responsibilities of spiritual stewardship. Do I resent this? No! I have come to understand that these things come with the territory. Sometimes women in such leadership feel like they are on show to the whole world. They feel like they are living in a glass house with everyone watching. They resent the challenge of being in a public position and have trouble negotiating opinion and criticism. Well, to be honest, this is one of the price tags attached to leadership, and God has certainly made provision for those of us in this position. Too often we can expend precious energy fighting battles that were never intended to be battles. They are simply challenges which God's abundant grace has made provision for. Decide that you are not going to allow challenges that come your way to keep you in enemy territory.

Don't Allow Challenges to Keep You in Enemy Territory

I have learned over the years that nothing goes unseen by God. He is very familiar and up to date with our lives. He sees our beginnings and our ends, and everything in between. In Hebrews 12–13, Jesus is described as the Author, Source, and Finisher of our faith. He is the one who first drew us into the race; He's the one who runs along beside us; He's the one who waits on the finish line. I don't know about you, but that makes me feel very secure. So when I consider this, one doesn't have to be a genius to work out that God must be very familiar with the challenges of my individual "running lane." That revelation caused the psalmist to write, "O LORD, you have searched me [thoroughly] and have known me. You know my downsitting and my uprising; You understand my thought afar off. You sift and search out my path and my lying down, and You are acquainted with all my ways" (Ps. 139:1–3 AMPLIFIED BIBLE).

I am reminded of an incident many years ago when Brian and I were traveling in the Australian outback. The roads were long and boring and I was daydreaming about home. Suddenly I sensed that the people at home were praying for us. With that, Brian slowed down and pulled our vehicle towards the verge of the road for no apparent reason. As I thought to myself, *Why is he doing that?*, a truck came careening around the corner on our side of the road. Brian had felt a strong urge to pull over. Thank God he responded. All I can remember is then thinking, *God knew that challenge was around the corner.* His grace provided for us in that He possibly made some dear saint at home pray for us, and heaven no doubt dispatched an angel to whisper in Brian's ear, "Pull over, son."

Without a doubt, God knows every bend and curve of our journey, and gives us grace for every circumstance. Our error comes into play when we do not recognize challenges for what they are. Instead of responding correctly and overcoming with the grace available to us, we inadvertently turn them into enemy ammunition. We allow molehills that should have been squashed underfoot to become mountains in our lives and we allow the enemy in. Peter describes Satan as one who "walks about like a roaring lion, seeking whom he may devour" (1 Pet. 5:8). Learn to live your life in such a way that when the enemy looks at you, he sees a sign that says "You *may not* irritate, harass or devour this woman!"

As we look at the breadth of challenges that today's woman faces, there are many "running lanes." Each lane is unique and wonderful, and ranges from the ultra-busy woman, to the woman who finds herself seemingly alone, to the lonely woman, to the hurting woman, to the woman in Christian leadership and ministry. I cannot possibly address them all fully, but here are a few thoughts that may help bring perspective.

The Ultra-Busy Woman

The corporate, career, or working woman faces immense challenges. If such a woman decides to give her best to her company or career, then there will be challenges upon her family, her leisure time, and even her health. As a working woman, she will face the pressure of running a home and working extended hours. Huffing and puffing or being resentful won't help the situation. She needs to come to an understanding that if this is her chosen course (or her chosen conviction), then by wisdom, discipline, and clever planning she can negotiate the challenges so they do not become enemies.

My life moves fast and I cannot escape that phenomenon. People may call me Pastor Bobbie, but I fall into this category. I am a full-time working woman. I have three kids, two dogs, and a husband who doesn't *walk* through life—he *zooms* through life. We lead a large and expansive church with numerous extension ministries and, in recent years, have been granted the awesome privilege of leading and hopefully influencing other denominations and fellowships in our nation. We travel extensively. I am married to a choleric-sanguine personality who, if *he* has an hour or two free, loves to drop everything and take off to play somewhere (too bad about the fifty loads of laundry that need to be done before he flies off the next morning). I love my home and my children and their friends are always welcome, but like every woman, I can get frustrated if the pressures of life squeeze out the time needed to keep house and home in order.

So it is to no one's advantage (especially my family's) for me to frown, pout, snarl, whine, complain, make everyone's life miserable, behave like a "dripping tap," and then collapse into a heap because I cannot negotiate the pace. If the pace belongs with the process, there has to be an answer. I have to rethink, reevaluate, rediscipline, perhaps redefine, and work smarter! (And find those handmaidens that Proverbs 31 talks about!)

Many years ago, Brian came to me one day and said he was taking on a new responsibility. I quietly and submissively said, "Honey, are you nuts? Seriously, how are you going to add another thing to your already maniac let's-see-if-we-can-kill-ourselves schedule?" His answer—"Work smarter!" He believed this added responsibility was part of our calling, so he felt that the challenges it would bring into our schedules would be met and overcome.

The "Seemingly Alone" Woman

How about our precious friend who says, "But I'm divorced?" As a pastor addressing other women in leadership, I need to say something here. We have entered the twenty-first century. Divorce has woven itself into the fabric of society and is a fact of life for many families. There is a harvest of souls about to be swept into the kingdom of God and a huge percentage of them will carry the effects or scars of divorce. God's heart is not to condemn—His heart is always to embrace! If you find yourself ministering to beautiful women who now find themselves in seasons of being alone, help them recognize the challenges that now belong to what has become the journey of their lives.

I have some awesome friends (sharp, articulate, stunning women) who now find themselves alone. They are raising their children alone; they are having to make financial decisions alone; they are having to discover the will of God for their family alone. Do they like their circumstances? No. Was this their expectation when they walked down the aisle? No. But they realize this has become, for now or however long, the process of their journey. My friends are becoming wise women, because they are deciding that these changed conditions are mere challenges that cannot be escaped. So rather than going into ostrich-mode, sticking their heads in the sand and pretending or wishing it wasn't happening, they are overcoming instead. Bravo girls! If you are such a woman, be encouraged. God definitely has plenty of grace to cover your world.

One of my friends shared a great story with me. Her child's father decided to disappear rather than meet the commitment he'd made to his family. The child was distressed and thought his daddy had died. But rather than succumb to this challenge and allow resentment and bitterness to take root, my friend took hold of God and His grace. She felt God's response to her was, "I'll be your child's father. I'll fill the gap in his life; trust Me." My friend could so easily have turned this challenge of being a solo parent into very dangerous territory for both herself and her child. Instead, she covered herself with something much better, the grace of God. In your church programming, be sure to teach such women how to grow and succeed. Teach them how to prosper financially, according to God's way. When there is no man in their lives, teach them how to hear God's voice and know His will for them. We have a responsibility to help these gorgeous and important women be such that others also look and say, "Gee, if she can do it, so can I. I'll have what she's having!"

Jesus takes care of every possible twist and bend in our lives. The Word tells us to "[always] treat with great consideration and give aid to those who are truly widowed (solitary and without support)" (1 Tim. 5:3 AMPLIFIED BIBLE).

The Lonely Woman

Is loneliness a challenge or an enemy? It can affect women from all walks of life and can be a very real issue for many people. The book of Proverbs so beautifully says that there are friends in this crazy old world who stick closer than brothers (Prov. 18:24). Our challenge is to find such friends.

Connecting with God and with a healthy church community can and does negate loneliness. But if people do not see loneliness as a challenge to be met and overcome, it can easily allow despair into our lives. Despair is potentially very destructive. It can cause us to lose hope. When we lose hope, total desperation can take root. People suffering extreme despair can do crazy things. The incidence of youth suicide in the southern hemisphere is among the highest in the world. Youth (and adults alike) take their own lives because challenges have remained unmet, unconquered, and have turned self-destructive. Christ died a painful death to carry the challenges of humanity, and the church of Jesus Christ on the earth today has a serious responsibility to provide people with the answers to life. Our goal is for everyone to arrive at their destination, unscathed and all in one piece.

I was "born again" in the Jesus Revolution of the 1970s. This revolution hit America in a big way and became headline news. A similar move of God happened in New Zealand at the same time. I remember being so passionate about my newfound faith that had stickers all over my school bag that said "Jesus Is the Answer." Well that statement is more than a cute Jesus Revolution slogan; it is life-changing truth that sets people free. The church needs to become stronger at communicating Jesus Christ into people's lives because He is the answer! The awakening that came with the Jesus Revolution of the 1970s has matured, and what we are witnessing today is a generation (both young and old) who are concerning themselves with the condition and plight of humanity. If you open your spiritual ears and listen carefully, the earth is trembling with the sound of revival—revival that will bring answers to the many injustices that only the grace and goodness of God can successfully address.

The Hurting Woman

Hurt is another challenge that can negatively affect any one of us if we so choose. How many people allow their hurts to walk them down a road to bitterness? Bitterness, unharnessed, has the power to defile many and even destroy some. The Word warns strongly about bitterness. In Hebrews 12:15, Paul writes about how the "root of bitterness springing up causes trouble" (NASB). My husband has often remarked that the one thing he remembers from Bible college was a lecturer saying, "Never develop a wounded spirit in life." What a gem of wisdom.

Can you see why challenges need to be met and overcome in our lives? If you are a leader, teacher, or pastor, can you see how important it is to teach people how to actually meet the challenges of their lives so that a hurting person does not become bitter? Salvation is one thing; transforming new believers into disciples is quite another.

The Woman in Ministry

Speaking from pastoral experience, it is so easy to confuse the challenge of leadership for the enemy. Leading people is very rewarding, but it can sometimes make you a little crazy (and I say that with the utmost affection). I find it amusing that God calls us "sheep." Sheep sometimes forget that the shepherds only want the best for them. They bleat and baa when the shepherd is trying to lead them to better pastures (*change*). They do not realize that the fresh pasture will make them bigger and better sheep (*blessing*). They wander off course and then won't cooperate when the shepherd tries to get them back on course (*destiny*). They need to understand that the shepherd is actually commissioned and anointed by God, and responsible before Him to perceive danger, such as wolves that are waiting to devour isolated sheep.

We are all in the process of growth. We are all working with our human natures, which are in the process of becoming redeemed human natures. When pastoring God's beautiful people, do not get confused or frustrated by the challenges of human nature. The people aren't the enemy. So who is the real enemy? As women in leadership who carry responsibility for others, we need to fine-tune our discernment so we can clearly recognize the real enemy—Satan.

Gird your sword
PRINCESS WARRIOR!
(and don't forget to smile!)

{ PSALM 45:3 }

CHAPTER EIGHT

Recognize the Real Enemy

I f you are blessed to find yourself in leadership, wise up! Wise up to the fact that there are real enemies to contend with from time to time, and if you start to become a blessing on the earth, and if your life begins to affect others in a positive way, then do not be surprised or dismayed when you encounter opposition. Satan would love to have the church distracted. As your church (wherever it might be) unites and begins to actually go outside the barn and do serious damage to the kingdom of darkness, then do not be surprised or dismayed if you encounter our adversary in all his wrath.

One of the most important portions of Scripture given in this area would have to be Ephesians 6:12–18. If you are serious about being a successful woman in leadership, then read these verses carefully. Listen to the incredible wisdom and strategy God is giving.

> For we are not wrestling with flesh and blood [contending only with physical opponents] but against the despotism,

against the powers, against [the master spirits who are] the world rulers of this present darkness, against the spirit forces of wickedness in the heavenly (supernatural) sphere.

Therefore put on God's complete armor, that you may be able to resist and stand your ground on the evil day [of danger] and having done all [the crisis demands], to stand [firmly in your place].

Stand therefore [hold your ground] having tightened the belt of truth around your loins, and having put on the breastplate of integrity and of moral rectitude and right standing with God,

And having shod your feet in preparation [to face the enemy with the firm-footed stability, the promptness and the readiness produced by the good news] of the Gospel of peace.

Lift up over all the [covering] shield of saving faith, upon which you can quench all the flaming missiles of the wicked [one].

And take the helmet of salvation and the sword the Spirit wields, which is the Word of God.

Pray at all times (on every occasion, in every season) in the Spirit, with all [manner of] prayer and entreaty. To that end keep alert and watch with strong purpose and perseverance, interceding on behalf of all the saints (God's consecrated people). (Eph. 6:12–18 AMPLIFIED BIBLE)

Amazing verses aren't they? When you are rocking your baby to sleep in the small, wee hours of the night and all is calm and beautiful, it's hard to imagine God was serious about such verses. When you and the kids are squashed up together on the lounge, laughing at some crazy sitcom or movie on television, it's hard to visualize such principalities and powers. When you walk along a beautiful beach and all is perfect, it's difficult to comprehend such an adversary. When you window-shop with friends and laugh over cappuccino and croissants, or when you snuggle up at night in a soft, safe bed, it's hard to believe in a hell-bent spiritual adversary who is out to destroy you.

For a moment though, consider the tear-stained faces of women and children battered and bruised from abuse. Consider the stark faces of those in our war-torn and ravaged nations. Consider the garbage bins around this world full of aborted children. Consider for a moment the lines of despairing men and women looking for jobs, when Jesus paid the price for their spiritual and natural prosperity. Consider the beautiful, fresh-faced young person who does not know how to respond to drugs, sex, or life because they have had no decent role models in their lives.

The moment you as an individual Christian or you as a church begin to take care of your own houses, overcome your own challenges, and dare to turn your stories into testimonies, you become the target of the enemy. The moment we start getting our acts together and set our sights on the Father's business of redeeming and healing broken humankind, we step into enemy territory. And my experience is that the enemy—the adversary, Satan, Lucifer, devourer, thief, deceiver of mankind—does not like it!

These verses in Ephesians talk about standing. As I mentioned in the beginning of this book, at the close of one of our Hillsong Leadership Conferences, many people came and thanked us for standing firm, despite a season of opposition. What was evident was that many had experienced a similar year as us, and because we had chosen to remain on course, it gave them great courage.

Emerge from the Shaking

The storms of life are not continuous, but hey, they are definitely part of the package. Nature gives us a variety of weather patterns, but every now and then a calm may be felt before a major storm breaks. Storms come and storms pass. Storms, however, can do some damage if things are not firmly secured.

My husband comes from Wellington, New Zealand, which is supposedly one of the windiest cities in the world. To compensate, all the trees in Wellington have incredible root systems so they do not blow over. (They also joke that you know you are in Wellington when you see the seagulls flying backwards.) God desires us to get firmly planted like those trees, so that nothing has the power to blow us over: "and having done all [the *crisis* demands] to stand [firmly in your place]" (Eph. 6:13 AMPLIFIED BIBLE).

I feel compelled to share with you principles learned from what had the potential to be a crisis in our journey. It was a seasonal situation and lasted about six months. The latter half of 1995 saw our own church experience a shaking. What I am discovering is that, lo and behold, God did a whole lot of shaking around this time all over the world. God promises that anything that can be shaken will be shaken, so friend, do not become undone because you feel the earth move. Our concern should be that if we find ourselves undone, it will prove that we were not as well-rooted and well-grounded in our conviction as we perhaps thought.

Allow me to share some background. In July 1995, we witnessed a wonderful leadership conference. It was our ninth conference, and in our nation and in our context of influence, to put it not so delicately, we put the wind up the devil! For some divine reason, God has blessed us with favor in this conference. It is a local church leadership conference that transcends denomination and culture, and for more than twenty years, people have traveled from all over the world to be part of it. It covers every conceivable aspect of church life and, in a nutshell, exists to champion the cause of the local church—not just our own church, but the churches of those who attend. No wonder the devil hates it!

At this conference, we enjoyed an incredible time of teaching, praise, and worship. Many lives and many churches were impacted. Stories would flood into our offices of churches and towns being turned upside down with a renewed spirit. Brian and I took a week after the conference to tie up loose ends and then we headed off for a little holiday with some friends. (I think God was just being terribly kind to give us a rest, because He knew what lay around the next bend.) We came home a week later, refreshed and ready to see everyone, and stepped off the plane where, literally, all hell broke loose with one of our key team players. It was the first time that something like this had happened to us. (In hindsight, prior to that conference I had sensed something brewing, and had called all our pastors' wives to prayer.)

At the time, our Hills congregation had experienced twelve wonderful years as a local church. There were a few challenges along the way, which are normal when you pioneer a church, but it was almost a honeymoon period. We had a great church, great people, great team, incredible doors of opportunity, lots of fun and laughter, blue skies, and plenty of cappuccinos to rejoice over. This challenge turned out to be a hard six-month season in what had so far been an incredible journey over many years.

Over the next several months it was as though demons came out of the woodwork on every front. When attacks come from every side, it is a sure sign that you are doing something right (which is contrary to some people's beliefs). We experienced a barrage of attacks—cancer, accidents, stinking-thinking, people throwing in the towel, isolated disloyalty in our team that disappointed our hearts, devil-induced confusion, opposition, and a fine thread of a "cancerous attitude" bent on contaminating and taking out this particular part of the body of Christ.

Paul wrote to Timothy with solemn passion about such contamination in the body of Christ amid great persecution and intense opposition from men who sought to hurt Redemption's plan. Paul was, in many ways, handing the baton on to Timothy and the future generations of which we are part. What he shares is extremely important if we are to effectively lead our churches and ministries into their full destiny. In this letter, Paul says much about discord, and describes discord among the brethren as a cancer that spreads like gangrene. (Fairly strong words, you would agree). He says, "But avoid all empty (vain, useless, idle) talk, for it will lead people into more and more ungodliness. And their teaching [will devour it] will eat its way like cancer or spread like gangrene" (2 Tim. 2: 16–17 AMPLIFIED BIBLE). He goes on to say those who fall victim to vain, useless, idle talk will miss the mark and swerve from the truth, and that such talk has the capacity to undermine the faith of others.

Don't Go Into Battle Naked

Let me share with you as a woman in leadership, who loves the Church of Jesus Christ with all her heart. When you are in spiritual leadership, there will be specific spiritual enemies to that leadership. If you aim to take on the enemy, you had better be great at wearing your armor because this adversary is ruthless. He does not care where or who he hits, as long as it hurts. Satan fights like a terrorist, aiming at the weak and innocent. When this adversary attacks, it is essential to know who you are in Christ and what the weapons are at your disposal. When someone precious to you is facing a life-threatening situation, you need to know how and where to draw faith and strength. Should someone stumble, you need to know how to pray and see grace written across the doorposts. Should lies and false accusations come against you, you need to know how to silence those voices, and when all manner of opposition and storms rise against you, you need to know how and where to stand firm.

For us, 1995 was a somewhat eventful year, but in retrospect, we would not exchange the experience. Our God proved Himself strong on our behalf, our church was strengthened, and together the majority of us advanced to become the people we are today. Two things happened in this season of growth for us.

The Enemy Will Attack

First, Satan attacked. Without a doubt, we were a threat to his destructive agenda. Our Heavenly Father wanted to bring salvation and life to humanity and our church was committed to this same purpose. Our people are full of God and full of vision, and are a company of dedicated, devoted, and servant-hearted people. Their desire is to see humanity rescued from death and destruction, and they will do whatever it takes to achieve that end. When you truly love something, you will give yourself to it and every decision and choice is subject to that commitment. As a local church, we long to see men, women, and precious young people delivered into the beautiful, abundant life God promises. As a church, devotion to this cause is not an issue. It is the same passion that carried Jesus to a lonely cross at Calvary, reminding us that, "Greater love has no one than this, that he lay his life down for his friends" (John 15:13 NIV).

Hillsong Church is also a church marked with a spirit of gladness. "Serve the LORD with gladness," declares Psalm 100:2 (NASB). Gladness, joy, excitement, and enthusiasm are all qualities which I marvel at in our people and are qualities that I have witnessed my husband sow into our ministry team over the years. This spirit of commitment and this spirit of joy and gladness came under attack during this season.

God Will Clean House

The second thing that happened to the "Class of 1995" was that God cleaned house. Funny that He should do that, but then again it is His house! Anything that can be shaken will be shaken and His Word declares that both the righteous and the wicked will be shaken. Do not know about you, but I'd much rather be counted with the righteous!

I think that God put our church through the fire just to see what it was made of. I have a shepherd's heart, and it broke my heart to see precious friends exposed to the test, but one day God spoke to me and said, "Bobbie, I have to put them through it. Be calm, I am bigger in their hearts than the fire." I also remember a dear, trustworthy friend saying prior to this shaking, "Brian, your church is on the edge of something powerful. Opportunity, success, and influence are in view. What is in the people's hearts will now be revealed."

The furnace is a refining fire, a purifying fire. It gets rid of the nonsense, the garbage, the dross, the chaff, the facade, and the baggage that prevents Christians reaching their fullest potentials. The fire is a good thing—painful at the time, but anyone worthy of his or her calling experiences it. Individuals (and churches) desiring to be "vessels of honor" have no choice. The fire exposes impurity and delivers the pure article. Twelve months later, our church and the subsequent Hillsong Leadership Conference were testimonies that God is faithful and God is true. We celebrated increase and blessing on all fronts. A decade or so has since passed, and with each year we have seen God take us from strength to strength (see Ps. 84).

Brian and I and the wonderful team around us, discovered during this season that, without a shadow of doubt, God had birthed our church, is building it, and He will continue to build it. Why such confidence? Because it does not belong to us, it belongs to Him! As a believer in the body of Christ, can you comprehend how wonderful that is? We also humbly recognize that God has allowed our church to contribute in bringing a new sound from heaven to earth in these exciting and significant days. For many years now our worship has gone across the earth and seems to carry to listening hearts the presence of God. The worship that is captured on these live albums is simply a reflection of a healthy and flourishing church in Australia. God has taken it and almost like a spearhead causes it to find its way into the remotest corners of the earth. Worship can pierce the hardest ground and then, if hearts dare to enquire, the arrow carries with it a greater message about the house of God. As I said before, Hillsong Church exists to champion the cause of the local church. In 1995, God took the spearhead, placed it in the fire, refined its edge, and entrusted to us an even greater world platform.

Our Heart for You

As strange as this may sound, we love your church and sincerely desire only the best for it. If you are familiar with our worship, then just listen to the lyrics. They reflect the heart and spirit of God and His Word, and they reflect the heartbeat of what I've been writing. The lesson that I am passing on is that your church is God's church too, and He will build it.

God loves people and has chosen to use us to establish His will on the earth; however, at the end of the day, it does not depend solely upon any specific individual. If it did, the church would be in a sorry state because for many good reasons, people come and go. In any church, God's kids can prove to be difficult. They may resist growth, change, and maturity. They may even rebel and dislocate themselves from the place where former conviction had them planted. If that is their choice, so be it. I do not think there would be a church anywhere that has not experienced this somewhere in the journey.

The Word describes such behavior as foolish, but the body will continue to grow, even despite a missing limb or two. God said He will build His church and, ultimately, He will have His way. It may take longer that we hope or the process may be prolonged and may disappoint His heart, but He will have His way. He will establish His church, despite spiritual opposition and uncooperative human nature.

Of course, those in leadership must do everything possible to prevent such tragedy, but the final analysis comes down to individual choice. There is an old saying, "You can lead a horse to water, but you can't make it drink." In Luke 15, the Word talks about people who get lost along the way:

- Some are lost because they just wander off course. It is not necessarily the shepherd's fault; they just wandered off and the Word tells us to look for them and to bring them back.

- Some are lost due to negligence. May none of us be guilty of this. May we all apply godly leadership principles and have sensitive hearts, so we do not ignore or neglect those in our realm.

- Others are lost because they willfully walk away. The Word equates them to the "prodigal son." They won't come home until they have come to their senses.

For those who return to the church, we should take the same attitude as the prodigal son's father. We should run and greet them, kiss their faces, book the best restaurant in town, and then take great joy in filling them in on all they had missed while they were out messing around in the world. I find it reassuring to know God has His church planted all over this wonderful planet. We find it on every continent, in different nations, throughout countless cities, and upon innumerable street corners. Every church faces similar challenges, but take courage, because if hearts are willing and teachable, He will perfect His perfect will in all of us.

CHAPTER NINE

Guard the Specifics

A large and flourishing church is similar in a number of ways to a large and prospering company. The leadership principles in this chapter can be applied to both. But it's important to note that we do not see our people as clients; we call them a congregation. They are God's beautiful children, and should be treated and respected with the utmost dignity. We do not measure success in profits; we measure success in lives changed and influenced in a positive way. The motive behind customer service flows from God's heart to love people and serve humanity, and the concept of a mission statement to achieve one's vision is universally understood. In our case, two areas—the head and the heart of our church—have come under attack in the past.

Heads and Hearts

Every church has a spiritual head. If you understand God's delegated authority and how the body of Christ works, you will understand that the spiritual head of each church is the Senior Pastor and his partner. They are appointed by God to be shepherds over your soul. Distract, disillusion, demoralize, or destroy the shepherd and it is very likely the sheep will scatter.

If sheep didn't need shepherds, God would have structured it differently. Sheep can be incredibly vulnerable sometimes. I originally come from New Zealand, which boasts a population of forty million sheep. They are very funny creatures to watch. They're born to follow, so if one jumps, they all jump. If they fall over, they often cannot get up. They just lie there with their cute little hooves in the air, looking helpless. They need love, care, green pasture, and they need to be led with strength. Mind you, they are very adorable (especially when they are lambs), and what is produced from their lives (wool) is quite spectacular. But sheep need a leader, and so do we.

Every church also has a heart. The heart, or soul, of a church is that company of people who make up the core. It is the leadership team along with the committed die-hards, those amazing people who carry the vision with the leadership. When the head (the senior pastors) or the heart (the leadership core) is negatively affected, then the whole church will be affected as well, even destroyed in some cases. So be wise here because Satan is no fool and the pages of history are littered with churches that have become casualties because of this.

To present it another way, if someone walked in right now and tried to kill you, they would be most effective if they aimed and shot you straight in the heart or the head. (I know this is a bit gruesome, but it illustrates the point.) However, if they only got you in the kneecap, you'd still be able to get around, albeit with a limp. If blew your right hand off (ouch!), you'd still live, and you would learn to write with your left hand. However, take the head or the heart out and we have a major problem—death.

Without a doubt, Satan did attack our church, and he did try to grow a cancer in the heart of our beautiful church. However, he failed miserably (hallelujah!) because we chose to stand strong, and we guarded these specific areas: we stood in faith, we refused to quit, we put on the armor, and we helped one another get our armor on perfectly. Ultimately, we remained focused, determined, and unshakeable! When he tried to attack the head of our church, it didn't work either. Honesty, transparency, accountability, integrity, character, and hearts determined to stay focused rose within us and we would not succumb! I want to honor my husband for his wisdom and integrity over this period. He stood strong despite personal loss, unfair lies, and innuendo. He remained a true leader. Contrary to "vain, idle and useless talk" (see 2 Tim. 2:16), he fought to rescue and restore people who were allowing themselves to be distracted, and he fought to forge_on for everyone else, never losing sight of the call, the destiny, and the purpose. I personally feel that what was designed by hell to sabotage our ministry, which is precious in God's sight, was diffused because these principles were applied.

I share these experiences with you because life is short; people are going to hell before our very eyes, and if Brian's and my story can give hope to others in leadership, then for that reason alone I gladly share it. Some of you will recognize your own experience here and say, "Amen Bobbie, that's right!" For others this will be light in your darkness and will bring hope to activate your faith, and for yet others still, this will be 'preventative wisdom' to hold and draw upon in days to come.

I initially penned the majority of these thoughts over a seven day period, and then the busyness of life pushed this book to the bottom of the drawer. After nine months I asked the Lord, "Should I continue this? Was this just an exercise so I could journal my experience, or do You really want me to finish this project?" Two days later God spoke prophetically through a person who had no idea about our lives, experiences, or influence as a ministry. Amid seven things that were too accurate for coincidence, the Lord commanded me, "Write the book, woman of God, write the book . . . make a recording of what you have birthed in this house, so that it will be a training manual for those who have lost their hope. Write the book, woman of God, and it shall be a memorial for your children to follow." I guess that was a definite "Yes!" to my request.

Now, how did that person know to encourage the writing of this book? At that point, nobody had even seen this project, which is typical of me. I am ambitious when it comes to the things of God, but not ambitious when it comes to promoting myself. So how did the prophet know? She knew because she had an acute ear to God's heart. There is a God in heaven who loves us and He wants us to love and help one another. I am here to be obedient to God. And I want to stand and cheer you on in your faith.

Yes, we do have enemies and yes, they will confront us from time to time. But this is the fantastic part: when we are in Christ, standing with His armor activated, they will not prevail! A long-time friend and respected minister from South Africa arrived into our world as the "War of 1995" kicked in. As he stepped off the plane and into our car, he proceeded to speak the anointed love and word of God to us. At one point, he quoted the Scripture we all know well, "No weapon formed against you shall prosper" (Isa.

54:17). Then our dear friend and kingdom-peer knelt down beside us and, tapping Brian's knee, said, "Now Brian, the weapon has been formed, but understand . . . it will *not* prosper." (I love my husband. He told me afterward that Ray's word relieved and depressed him all at the same time.) That season effectively taught us to guard the soul of our endeavor. Your soul consists of a mind, a will, and emotions. Your church also has a soul. It also has a mind, a will, and emotions. Do not forget I am sharing from our ministry-platform, but these principles can apply to many aspects of life. There are three things to remember: keep the mind of your church healthy, keep the will of your church alive, and keep the emotional state of your church healthy.

Keep the Mind of Your Church Healthy

Keep the mind and the thinking of your church renewed. Do not allow stinking-thinking and incorrect attitudes to take root. Keep your leadership healthy. Stay in their lives; stay in their faces; give them clarity, hope, and direction; keep the vision alive. "Write the vision, and make it plain" (Hab. 2:2 KJV). Without clear vision, people dwell carelessly and can even perish (Prov. 29:18). Responsible leadership committed to stewardship will not passively tolerate sin, negative attitudes, or stinking-thinking, all of which have the power to infiltrate. God in His wisdom tells us that a little leaven leavens the whole lump. Remember that the health of your church (or ministry or company) flows from the head down. Keep every aspect healthy.

As a woman in leadership, play your part. You are in partnership here. In the animal kingdom, there is nothing more moving and powerful than a mother protecting her young under threat. When I saw the enemy picking on our people (those entrusted into our care), something very protective rose within me. My attitude was, "Devil, you want to contend with someone, contend with me! Come on, I dare you." I thank God that the Class of 1995 taught me how to "wield the sword." I am seriously not afraid of the devil and I will fight! I thank God for a church full of people who know how to pray. We certainly did not stand alone. I thank God for such people who have confidence in the integrity of their leadership, and know how to trust both when they understand and when they do not understand.

I thank God for my own personal relationship with the Lord. In the midst of what seemed our darkest hours, I remember sitting on our balcony. It was a beautiful day—the sky was blue, the air still, with the Australian gum trees in our backyard swaying in the breeze. I remember sitting there on this beautiful, calm, perfect day, looking up into the sky and thinking, It is so calm in the natural, but there is a spiritual storm raging against us in the heavenlies. I remembered a verse in *The Message* that I had read that week (see, it's good to read your Bible). It said to give God "your warmest smile" (Ps. 34:5). So there on that beautiful, still spring day, I chose to rise above the raging spiritual storm and I literally gave God my warmest smile. A big, fat, cheesy one! And, do you know what? I think I sent the devil ballistic. Can you imagine him and all his cohorts perched on my balcony rail— "No! No! You're not supposed to smile! You're not supposed to be smiling! You're supposed to be discouraged! You're supposed to be dismayed! You're supposed to be throwing in the towel, not smiling! Don't smile! It's not working! We can't stand that!"

Live a lifestyle of resistance. *Resist the devil and he shall flee.* Smile, and you'll make that old enemy crazy every time: "So be subject to God. Resist the devil [stand firm against him], and he will flee from you. Come close to God and He will come close to you" (James 4:7 AMPLIFIED BIBLE). I believe soldiers who smile, athletes who smile, and farmers who smile are pretty irritating to our adversary.

I will add that the aspect of the attack that was directed personally at Brian and me did not actually consume our thoughts. Our darkest moment was in the knowledge that the "cancerous thread" that threatened, if left unrestrained, had the capacity to hurt a lot of innocent people. It had the capacity to thwart their potentials and their God-given destinies, which is enough to make any true shepherd rise to the battle!

Keep the Will of Your Church Alive

Brian has taught a lot about the will to live, the will to succeed, and the will to serve. This is a powerful truth. Your church (like our church) has a specific vision, purpose, and predestined plan, which God wants you to achieve. Jesus. in Matthew 6:9–13 taught us how to achieve this. He told us to pray to Our Father in this way: "Your will be done on earth as it is in heaven" (NIV). Keep the vision, or the will of God, for your church alive, come hell or high water. I watched my husband keep the dream, the vision, the will of Hillsong Church alive when all hell was bent on destroying it. This is so important, because the dream affects the potential of multitudes of people. Take this attitude:

• I will stand firm in the will of God.

- I will not surrender the will of God.
- I will, for the sake of God's beautiful people, stay true
  to my call.

A love for God Himself and a love for His greater purpose will always give people strength to stand.

When I originally wrote these thoughts, I opened my Bible to the Lord's Prayer in Matthew 6 and I felt led to include it. The depth of these words are so magnificent. I wonder if you grew up like me, reciting this at school assembly. Even though it may be familiar, never take it lightly. The disciples asked Jesus to teach them how to pray. Read and embrace its power with me:

> In this manner, therefore, pray:
> Our Father in Heaven,
> Hallowed be Your name.
> Your kingdom come.
> Your will be done
> On earth as it is in heaven.
> Give us this day our daily bread.
> And forgive us our debts,
> As we forgive our debtors.
> And do not lead us into temptation,
> But deliver us from the evil one.
> For Yours is the kingdom and the power and the glory forever.
> Amen. (Matt. 6:9–13)

Now . . . did you absorb heaven's heart in these amazing verses? Isn't it awesome? In case this book, by some wild chance of providence, has found its way into the hands of an unbeliever who is seeking truth, or a person who is backslidden in heart, or a leader who has been wounded by circumstance, let me whisper something to you now: you can dedicate (or rededicate) your life to Christ on the wings of that prayer. Still your heart and ask Jesus into your life. Ask Him to forgive you and cleanse you, and give you His gift of life. Now thank Him and ask Him to lead you to a great church where you will discover how awesome it is to walk and grow with Jesus.

All of us can get wounded and hurt along the way. Life can deal some whoppers, but leadership demands we rise above hurt and keep going. It is a choice to remain hurt and wounded. Choosing to remain this way is to ignore the Savior who paid an enormous price to purchase our freedom. Women who are strong leaders rise up and keep going. The will to live (and serve) gets them up in the morning and moving because there are people to see, places to go, destinies to fulfill. The Word says His mercies are new every morning (Lam. 3:23), so take Him literally on this one. His mercies abound toward her as she jumps up in the morning, dives into the shower, makes herself look delicious-for-the-day, gulps down a coffee or herbal tea, and says, "Hallelujah! This girl has got people to see, places to go, and destinies to fulfill today!"

Keep the Emotional State of Your Church Healthy

Thank you, Father, for the joy of the Lord. The Bible tells us that it is our strength and it is not dependent upon circumstance and perfect conditions. A spirit of thankfulness and a spirit of gladness do wonders for the human heart. Stay happy, stay on top, talk to your soul, and command it to rejoice. Keep your church happy, stay victorious, talk to the heart of your church and lovingly command them to rejoice. I must admit from experience over the past years, that our church has an incredible capacity to rejoice and press on regardless of adversity.

Maintaining a buoyant spirit is a great key in leadership. This doesn't mean we are insensitive to difficult or trying situations, but rather strive to rise up again quickly. We need to learn to live our lives in such a way that opposition realizes we will not easily be contained or defeated. As a church, we have faced some funny challenges. How many people in life could say they've been hit by lightning? Not many. Our offices were hit twice during that challenging period of 1995. How many churches have had bomb threats? On the Sunday we recorded the praise song "Shout to the Lord" (which according to Integrity Music is sung by thirty to forty million Christians every week), we had to evacuate church in the middle of worship. Was there a stampede? No. We just smiled, raised our eyebrows at each other, grabbed coffee, and chatted in the sunshine as dozens of police searched the building. Sometimes the enemy must feel quite pathetic in his attempts to sabotage God's plans.

I do not actually spend a lot of time majoring on the devil, however, he was aggressively in our faces for a season, and will no doubt be in our faces again, as we move into exciting and crucial days. My attitude is "*In your face* devil . . . stick that in your pipe and smoke it!" If I wasn't a girl, I'd probably get off on that Clint Eastwood thing: "Go ahead . . . make my day!"

I'll just add one final testimony in this area, as it may help someone reading this. I remember toward the end of this trying period, my husband (who chose to obey God, shut his mouth, and allow God to vindicate us) momentarily became transparent about the issue at hand and exposed his human heart. Our church rose to their feet and applauded us. They clapped and clapped and clapped and clapped and clapped. We were overwhelmed by their awesome response and I distinctly remember sensing that it was a "spiritual clap." A spiritual clap that, in the spirit realm, drove away the darkness. Our church has always been fruitful, but from that moment, everything accelerated.

I then remember being on the phone to another pastor's wife in another city not long after this particular Sunday morning. She said, "Bobbie, it feels like all hell has broken out over here against our ministry." I remember looking out my window and saying, "Well girl, you know what? I think the devil has just packed up and moved cities, because the air feels really clear here again." I was able to encourage her from our experience and I trust I have been able to encourage you as well.

Negotiate your journey well. Clearly recognize and overcome challenges, and learn to deal victoriously with anything seeking to sabotage your destiny, because you have a big, beautiful life to live!

PART 4

BE A WOMAN OF CONVICTION

TION
ction

\con'vic'tion\, n.
belief, faith, persuasion, certainty,
intensity, power, vigour, force,
strength, fervour and passion

man of conviction

Christine Caine—Colour 2001 (photo by Femia Shirliff)

'Feminism in its purest origin is
the emancipation of wrongly
imprisoned womanhood'

CHAPTER TEN

Conviction, Calling, and the Cause

C onviction is possibly the most powerful force on the earth today. It is a belief that enables people to rise and achieve the impossible. It is the force that caused Jesus Christ to endure a brutal cross for our redemption. His all-consuming conviction was to restore lost humanity to His Father, and He commissioned His church to do likewise.

Being a woman of strong conviction has nothing to do with misguided feminism. Feminism in its purest origin is the emancipation of wrongly imprisoned womanhood. God loves women. He created us and has a master plan for each and every one of our lives. Jesus had plenty of friends who were women and these women held strategic and honored places in His heart, life, and ministry. His entire message was one of releasing wrongly imprisoned humanity, women included. Misguided feminism sometimes involves women trying to be men, when God created them women. Be assured that God has a brilliant attitude towards the female gender and has plenty for us to achieve.

A dear friend of mine wrote a book called *Woman! Get in Your Place*. Great title. At first glance, you might ask what she means by such a bold statement. Is that behind the kitchen sink or behind the executive desk? Is that behind a baby pram or behind the pulpit? Is that behind, beside, or in front of your man?

She means, "Woman, get in position!" Discover your purpose and understand that whatever it is, it is all worthy. There is no one as worthy as you to fill that position—no one can be mum to your child quite like you can. No one can stand beside and complete your husband like you. No one in the body of Christ can fill your individually designed position as perfectly as you. And when you understand the power of this, you will feel complete in yourself and find yourself complementing the big picture as well. I believe a woman of conviction will pursue an understanding of this truth, and once recognized and understood, she will quietly not allow anything to steal her passion. All of us can forfeit our destinies by refusing to grow and expand, by refusing to submit and be Christ-like, or by refusing to go to the next level.

Always be mindful of God's wisdom regarding growth and advancement, because none of these things happen overnight. James 1:4 reminds us to "let patience have its perfect work." Be patient with God. Trust Him with the time frames of your life and never forget that He's God and you're not. Be patient with others in the puzzle. Sometimes God cannot connect the adjoining puzzle piece because that adjoining puzzle piece is just not cooperating. God has to keep working on them, so we need to remain patient and not become frustrated. (Imagine a rebellious jigsaw puzzle piece, refusing to be placed on the board.) Be patient with yourself. Let peace govern your heart and as the Word says, allow peace to act as umpire, directing your steps. Your future will definitely unfold beautifully if you apply all these keys.

The apostle Paul understood conviction. His faith and belief enabled him to endure conditions that would have sent shivers down our spines. His faith and belief had him pressing on to achieve His purpose, regardless of opposition and circumstance. In the book of Timothy, he pleads with his spiritual son Timothy to carry in his heart the same conviction.

An Excellent, Exciting, and Most Worthy Cause

The revelation that you were born for a cause bigger than yourself opens up a world more wonderful than most of us can imagine. First Timothy 3:1 says, "The saying is true and irrefutable: If any man [eagerly] seeks the office of bishop (superintendent, overseer) he desires an excellent task (work)" (AMPLIFIED BIBLE). When God says something is excellent, simply believe what He says. So whatever you find yourself involved in, believe with every fiber of your sweet being that God has called you to a most excellent, most exciting, and most worthy cause! If your position in the puzzle of life is in the home, raising brilliant kids, then know without doubt that this is a most excellent, exciting, and worthy cause (and possibly the finest thing a mother can achieve). If your position in the puzzle of life is in business or career, then astound those around you with a work ethic that screams that this career or this business is a most excellent, exciting, and worthy cause. And if your position in this puzzle is in the honored and precious call of ministry, then allow conviction to enlarge the revelation that you are also involved in a truly excellent, exciting, and worthy cause!

In Hebrews 13:7, we are encouraged to learn from the lives of leaders whose lives are producing something good. We are told to observe and imitate the fruit and outcome of their well-spent lives. Do not passively observe and perhaps think, *I'd love to have what she's having,* but rather draw near enough to ask her, "What makes you tick?" A woman of conviction also refuses to lose ground unnecessarily. A lifetime can be spent establishing a home, a family, and a career, and the silliest of things can sabotage the end result. I pray that conviction will rise within you and always cause you to live above such tragedy.

My beautiful Laura—Summer 2002 (Photo by Bobbie Houston)

HEY SUNSHINE . . . 'Guard your HEART
with all diligence because out of it flow all the
ISSUES OF LIFE'

{ PROVERBS 4:23 }

CHAPTER ELEVEN

Hold Your Ground; Don't Give It Away

We have talked a lot about the importance of holding your ground, especially in the heat of spiritual battle, but we also need to learn how to hold our ground when there's no actual war in sight.

By simply not behaving as we ought to, especially on the days that are a just normal or unspectacular, we can lose ground so easily. You know the days I mean—the days when the most exciting thing you did was go to the mailbox; the days when the only people you encounter are the people you live with; the days when we sometimes forget who we are because we aren't wearing our Sunday best. It is usually the little issues of the heart that have the power to knock us off course, and if we are going to be effective women in leadership, then we need to guard these things.

I am very aware of the hundreds of people who watch my life. I want to live my life in such a way that I do not disappoint them. For that reason I need to understand the challenge and charge in 1 Timothy 3. I need to discover for example, what it is to live "resistant to accusation." I need to know the keys to "living above reproach," and I need to know how to remain self-controlled when life sometimes wants to make me lose control. Read the following verses carefully and allow me to share a few thoughts.

Now a bishop (superintendent, overseer) must give no grounds for accusation but must be above reproach, the husband of one wife, circumspect and temperate and self-controlled; [he must be] sensible and well behaved and dignified and lead an orderly (disciplined) life; [he must be] hospitable [showing love for and being a friend to the believers, especially strangers or foreigners, and be] a capable and qualified teacher, not given to wine, not combative but gentle and considerate, not quarrelsome, but forbearing and peaceable, and not a lover of money [insatiable for wealth and ready to obtain it by questionable means].

He must rule his own household well, keeping his children under control, with true dignity, commanding their respect in every way and keeping them respectful. For if a man does not know how to rule his own household, how is he to take care of the church of God?

He must not be a new convert, or he may [develop a beclouded and stupid state of mind] as the result of pride [be blinded by conceit and] fall into the condemnation that the devil [once] did.

Furthermore, he must have a good reputation and be well thought of by those outside [the church] lest he become involved in slander and incur reproach and fall into the devils trap. (1 Tim. 3:2–7 AMPLIFIED BIBLE)

Live Above Accusation

When it comes to accusation, our adversary is not the only one who can shoot fiery darts. Sometimes the unredeemed behavior of those closest to us can fire a few bullets. If you come under fire, conviction seeks an inner strength that says, "I can handle this. I'm not going to get all destroyed by what is happening." Conviction will cause someone to draw on their faith and examine their own hearts first. Then, if forgiveness is needed, they will seek that forgiveness. Forgiveness will always allow God room to move.

A woman with conviction takes responsibility for her own heart, keeping it pure, so no accusation can actually find legal ground in her life. Proverbs 26:2 says, "the curse causeless shall not come" (KJV). This may help you understand how important godly behavior is. Two types of armor are described in the Word. One type of armor is described as a shield of light. It refers to godly, Christ-like behavior. I love the Lord because He actually makes life very simple for us, yet so often we fail to understand. Basically, when we get our acts together, and behave in a manner that is correct, then this becomes a shield that has the ability to deflect darkness and save us a lot of pain. The concept isn't that difficult to grasp, but it's amazing how many of us miss it. The second type of biblical armor is found in Ephesians 6. It is used for fighting real spiritual forces. A woman of conviction will wisely wear both kinds of armor, so that nothing will affect, contain or rob her.

Live Above Reproach

A sharp woman of conviction recognizes that leadership carries a price tag. Basically our margin for error is reduced. Life should be fun and perish the thought that we cannot be ourselves, but our behavior needs to be sensible and well behaved. A responsible leader is always mindful of offending others, and would never intentionally put a stumbling block in front of anyone.

Live with Discipline

If you desire to succeed in life, it is pointless to try and avoid discipline. Discipline comes with the territory and it's worth noting that undisciplined soldiers often perish, undisciplined athletes usually lose, and undisciplined farmers miss the harvest. *Discipline* simply means to "be trained." Such a woman realizes that, first and foremost, the Word of God will effectively train her. She also realizes that life's experiences can train her, and she understands the importance of godly friends, who will steer her in the right direction. If you do not have godly friends, pray them in, and then never forget to be one yourself.

Live a Generous and Hospitable Life

Women with conviction regarding the bigger picture understand how important it is to be embracing and hospitable. Faith causes them to react beautifully and generously when, for example, that lovely husband brings home a few unexpected guests. Grace marks such a woman of God. When it comes to strangers and foreigners, conviction will cause you to rise above any shyness and insecurity, because often God uses such people to stretch our world. The planet is a big, bright, fabulous place and meeting such people always enlarges our worldview. The Bible also suggests we just better be nice also, because you never know when you might be entertaining angels unknown (Heb. 13:2). Now there's food for thought. How embarrassing to discover you'd just been rude to an angel?

Live as a Qualified Teacher

Leadership demands that a woman of conviction also becomes a qualified and capable teacher. She may never actually stand publicly and speak, but her life will teach others. Literally speaking, her very lifestyle will show others the way to go. God will use a variety of circumstances to stretch us, so we can develop into such women. I remember my Heavenly Father deciding it was time for me to step out of my safe little world and grow. He knew what lay ahead for me and knew that to achieve it, I had to grow.

So He picked me up, carried me to the other side of the planet, and gently dumped me in the midst of a bunch of strangers. They seriously intimidated me. (Even my wardrobe was intimidated; I borrowed clothes from all my friends for the conference we were attending). I felt sick as the plane landed. Behind my calm little facade, my seriously-challenged-comfort-zone was having a wee panic attack, *How come they're all so darn confident? Is this just an American thing or do they know something I do not know?* However it was this very confidence (the confidence of a bunch of strangers), that God had purposed would stretch and take me to new levels. I must add that these strangers have now become our dearest friends.

CHAPTER TWELVE

Conviction that Produces

Awesome women of God are productive. It is impossible to be filled with God and have nothing to show for it. Your life will display wonderful qualities that you will carry into every situation, room and conversation. First Timothy 3:3 – 7 throws a few challenges in our direction—qualities such as being not given to excess, not combative, gentle, considerate, not quarrelsome, forbearing, peaceable, not a lover of money, rules their house well, kids under control, dignified and respectful.

Hello . . . is this the woman you see in the mirror each morning? At least when it comes to leadership, we cannot say that we have got nothing to attain to. I believe the spirit of a conviction-driven woman has her seeking God's ways and His victory in every circumstance of life. I picture her becoming the "no-matter-what" kind of woman.

She Produces Contentment and Peace in Her Home

First Timothy 3:3 is literally talking about not being given over to wine, but having a sense of conviction will not allow this woman to be ruled by *any* form of excess. She is wise and understands the fine balance of desiring things, having things, and knowing when to be content. She will also produce this in her children and her sphere of influence. She is not a lover of money, but does have an understanding of healthy biblical prosperity, and knows that God desires us to be resourced in order that we can make a difference in the world.

This woman is not combative. She'll seek peace, no matter who is right or wrong. Now I do not know how you interpret that, but to me that is a big call. Can you and I do that in our own strength? I do not think so, not unless I was in the bathroom when they were handing out some special anointing. No, we cannot do that in our own strength, because unredeemed human nature loves to make things difficult, but as we exchange our strength for His strength and His mind for our mind, we will discover this amazing reality.

She Carries Peace Into Every Encounter

Wherever she walks, she is mindful of people watching. At times, I have felt the pressure of people watching. I pray, *But Lord, there are all these precious people watching our reactions and responses. They watch us sit, stand, scratch our heads. They watch us raise our kids, they watch body language, they watch when we are tired or stressed, they watch me overtake them when I'm running late for church—they watch everything. Help me Lord to live my life in such a way that You are glorified and honored.*

There have been times in my marriage when I didn't want to be the peacemaker. I wanted to choose war; I wanted to choose combat! I wanted to declare, "Not fair!" but everything inside me said, "Choose peace for the sake of the people." Now before you all vomit, you have to know that Brian and I, like every other married couple on the planet, have faced all the same wonderful challenges of having our flesh knit together over the past thirty years. The mark of leadership, however, is in the fact that your life is not your own and you have a responsibility to "get it right" for the sake of those watching. Some people do not want to hear that, but nevertheless, these are the facts.

Leadership is about bringing security to the people you lead. Many who follow are unable to deal with ugly, unredeemed displays of your flesh. They get shocked, hurt, or disappointed, and sometimes it is enough to send them off course. That is not stewardship. Of course, I am not talking about being unreal and putting on facades because people see right through that. I'll also add that onlookers should not be critical of leaders either—they are growing and changing like everyone else. Do not allow anything to bring division in your life. Division has the ability to separate us from the love of God, from one another, and from our destinies.

She Creates a Great Atmosphere Around Her

She is the "atmosphere queen," especially in her home, because she lives to rule her house well. This house relates to our natural homes and our own hearts. The atmosphere in our homes is actually determined by the condition of our hearts. Each room in our inner person needs to be subject to God's light. Do not leave any corner or rug unturned. People often walk in and out of God's will because they allow the Lord into some aspects of their lives, but not others. Then they wonder why one minute they're in the light and the next minute in darkness. It's like having only half the lights on in the house and perish the thought that anyone would look at us and say, "Yeah . . . only got half the lights on . . . do not think we'll have what they're having!" Bring everything into the light of Jesus Christ, because the enemy only has authority to traffic in darkness. Allow the Holy Spirit to search your heart and you'll stand strong, having authority to rule well in God's house because your own house is diligently taken care of.

She Seeks to Raise Brilliant Children

As parents, we have a God appointed responsibility to train our children correctly. Our responsibility is to teach our beautiful babies how to rule their own hearts. Training is a process. It is not a matter of telling them once and then becoming frustrated or furious because they haven't responded. Children need to be taught the rhyme and reason of life. Explain to them how life works. Explain why behavior has its consequences. Explain that obedience and good behavior brings reward, and disobedience and bad behavior brings correction. Badly behaved adults are just usually bigger versions of badly behaved children. They complain, sulk, whine, and often throw extremely unattractive adult-sized tantrums.

She Commits to a Pride-free Zone

This woman of conviction (she's quite a lady isn't she?) understands that pride is a stupid state of mind. Its undesired affect on people, according to the Word, causes them to become clouded in their thinking, which then leads to stupid mindsets. Pride is originally seeded by conceit, which is defined as having too high an opinion of oneself, and is perpetrated by forces contrary to the Lord. To live in humility and be an example of humility is a wonderful gift. I love God because He never waters down the facts. Far too many gifted, talented, and potential-laden people have sabotaged their destinies (and the potential of everyone within their influence, children included) simply because their heads got too big for their shoulders. As the childhood nursery rhyme teaches, "Humpty Dumpty (fat head) sat on the wall; Humpty Dumpty had a great fall." Pride always comes before a fall (Prov. 16:18).

She Produces a Good Reputation Around Her

Wherever her beautiful little feet go, she is very much the Proverbs 31 woman. Such delightful women should have the unchurched world observing and scratching their heads in bewilderment and even saying, "I wish I had what she has." Hopefully like you, I am still working on all these qualities, but I do recall my neighbor telling me about a comment her teenage daughter made. Whenever I would see them I would wave, smile, and love them as much as they would allow me. One day they apparently had a little conversation about me. "What makes Bobbie so happy, so free?" the mother asked. The young teenager apparently replied,

"Well mum, I think Bobbie is doing in life what she really wants to do, and it makes her happy." How tragic that so many people, for whatever reason, expend their energy and life on pursuits that really do not make them happy. Our wonderful challenge is to present godly perspectives that will help them find meaning and purpose in their own lives.

The Holy Spirit—Don't Ignore Him

Conviction can be defined as "possession, intensity, power, vigor, force, strength, fervor, and passion." One cannot help but recognize the attributes of the Holy Spirit here. I know many amazing women and the strength of their lives involves personality, background, input, and opportunity, but they each give place of honor to the person, presence, and power of the Holy Spirit. The Holy Spirit is revealed as both gentle and dynamic. He is the one who, we are told in the book of Genesis, hovered over something that was empty, without form, and covered in darkness. God Almighty spoke and They (the Father, Son and Holy Spirit) created the earth and all its awesome fullness. I am sure when They put their heads together and started creating, it would have been with intensity, power, vigor, force, strength, fervor, and passion. Imagine creating the planet and all its inhabitants? First Timothy 3:16 says, "[God] was made visible in human flesh, was *justified and vindicated in the [Holy] Spirit,* was seen by angels, preached among the nations, believed on in the world [and] was taken up in glory" (AMPLIFIED BIBLE, emphasis mine).

"Justified and vindicated by the Holy Spirit." Wow! Do not leave the dynamic of the Holy Spirit out of your life. As women, we may leave home without many things—our makeup and AmEx included—but let's never leave home without the presence of the Holy Spirit. In Exodus, Moses asked God what would distinguish His people, and then said that the people would not go on without it God's presence. The Holy Spirit will empower you because that is what the Father has commissioned the Him to do. He will invigorate you with times of refreshing. He will contend on your behalf and He will strengthen you with fervor and passion. His nature is to come alongside and reveal the heart and purpose of the Father to you and me.

I love the Holy Spirit, and as the days unfold, I am constantly finding Him a true Friend, a true Helper, and a true and faithful traveling companion. Are you beginning to feel inspired to stand firm in the conviction of your faith and destiny? I hope so.

PART 5

BE A WOMAN OF STRONG RESOLVE

RESOLVE

be a woman

\re'solve\, n.
purpose, intention, will, decision, determination, resolution

'Resolve has you seeking the
necessary tools and skills so you
can secure your own destiny'

of strong resolve

Finish the STORY beautiful lady!

CHAPTER THIRTEEN

Don't Settle for Half a Testimony

H aving conviction is one thing, but having the skill, determination, and resolve to maintain or secure that conviction so that it is unshakeable is another thing altogether. For centuries, the world has had a passionate love affair with the Olympic spirit. God also loves this spirit because He used the qualities of the athlete to teach us many parables about life, endurance, and victory. During the 1996 Atlanta Olympic Games, the Australian men's basketball team were defeated by the American Dream Team, the world's most daunting basketball machine. It was said of the Australian team, that they could have won because they had enough heart, passion, and cohesion. All that limited them was athletic prowess. They just need to grow taller and develop their already existing skill. Prowess means skill, expertise, valor, and gallantry.

I remember teaching our women about endurance. I exhorted them not to be women who settle for half the testimony, but rather be women who go for the whole testimony. You may sense the call of God on your life but the looming question is, "Are you on track in fulfilling that call?" The half-a-testimony woman could reply, "No, but I got offended along the way," or "It became too difficult," or "I couldn't muster the energy to go the distance." All of the above are what I call an unfinished testimony. Heaven longs to complete the good work that was begun in you (Phil. 1:6). A woman of strong resolve discovers what it takes to go the whole way.

The half-a-testimony person may say, "Oh, I've got this promise. I'm so excited. I have written it in the front of my Bible because I feel God has truly spoken." Wonderful, but here is the question again: "Have you secured that promise yet? Do you actually know how you are going to obtain it?" The half-a-testimony response could sound like this, "Well, no. I just figured in the fullness of time that it will fall out of the sky." Honey, nothing just falls from the sky, except maybe Australian birds in the outback heat. God expects us to be active in securing our promises, and what is even more amazing is that His Word has the capacity to equip us perfectly to obtain that inheritance and destiny.

Resolve has you seeking to finish the story. Resolve does not have you sitting at one point, wondering how on earth you are going to negotiate life so you can get to the next point. Resolve has you seeking, like the Aussie basketball team, the necessary tools and skills so that you can secure your own destiny. A number of years ago, I sensed what I believe was a divinely purposed God-whisper, "Bobbie, create a conference in Sydney, for women—predominately for younger women, but girded about with older, wise women—and tell them that there is a God in heaven who believes in them and a company of people believing in them also."

Sensing something like this is one thing, but knowing what to do with such a moment is another thing all together! There was no accompanying ten-year strategy with the whisper, just a clear prompting from God. To see the Colour Conference become the empowering story that it is has taken conviction, determination, and an ongoing commitment to a spirit of resolve.

Psalms 68:11 is a messianic psalm that speaks of a great host of women emerging in the last days who will carry the power and anointing of God. I am committed to gathering and raising such a company of women—women whose lives and stories, although not perfect, have nevertheless encountered the truth and grace of God and have risen strong. The Colour journey and the growing sisterhood of women I am witnessing across the earth is testimony to such a spirit. I pray that you also will find the inner resolve to rise up and become the woman God has called you to be. There are always others who need to hear and benefit from your story.

My gorgeous 'forever friend' Darlene
. . . pregnant and radiant

{ COLOUR 2001 }

CHAPTER FOURTEEN

Become an Agent of Resolve

Resolve is an amazing quality. It simply means to "make up one's mind." When I met the Lord at the tender age of fifteen, I made up my mind that I would love and serve Him no matter what that meant. Thirty five years later I am still determined to serve Him no matter what that means.

In 1997, the world mourned the passing of two exceptional women—Princess Diana and the delicate, legendary Mother Teresa. Like millions of others, I was impacted as I watched the world mourn. I could not help but feel that a powerful seed had fallen into the ground that week and that many people would be inspired to touch their worlds with similar compassion and kindness. Each of these women gave the best they could. They had each made up their minds to touch humanity, bring answers, and if it was within their capacity, to bring healing.

Resolve can be defined as "purpose, intention, will, decision, determination, and resolution"—all qualities of endurance that we have been talking about. Within the meaning of resolution we find qualities of kindness and blessing. One definition defines it as having the means to answer, explain, fix and make work again. These words paint a picture of a person with the capacity to be successful and influential. I dared to look up the word *capacity* and found within its meaning the descriptions of volume, character, ability, dimension, extent, magnitude, size, aptitude, brains, capability, cleverness and efficiency. (Phew! It is a little like going back to school isn't it?)

Well, I do not know what kind of person you are, but I love these words. They sound like the words of God to me. They remind me of all the qualities that God loves to spread abroad in our lives that enable us to be champions on the earth who embrace life and people, and who seek to bring light, love, and goodness wherever they go. Women of strong resolve want to find answers in their own experiences, so they in turn may bring answers to others. Imagine being such a woman. Imagine being so beautifully equipped and empowered that you were able to bring resolve to another person's challenge.

Mother Teresa literally used whatever was in her hand and Princess Diana did the same, but with much grander resource. We too can take whatever is in our hand, and believe it will bring healing to others. Imagine having a friend in need and your immediate response is, "I have the answer!" How awesome would that be? Imagine a friend or associate (or even a stranger) who does not understand their circumstance. Perhaps sickness, tragedy, or a difficult issue has come against them, but you, with godly insight, are able to say, "Perhaps I can explain that for you." Imagine being so beautifully anointed that you carry the ability to fix a hurting person's experience.

These are amazing thoughts and demonstrate the goodness of God finding expression in and through a person who is committed to resolve. This woman of resolve has become an exceptional person. She has learnt the art of successfully negotiating certain territory in her own experience, and her testimony may literally become the key that releases another. And perhaps it won't even be her personal testimony, but the testimony of one of her awesome, overcoming friends. This book is full of my friends' stories. For that reason we all need to connect in the house of God so that we can know and share the great things that God is doing in our lives.

Speaking of testimonies, I have a dear friend and colleague, Marilyn, whose story fits perfectly in this discussion. This friend is full of personality, pizzazz, fun, color, and talent—an infectious delight to be around. I doubt that anyone would ever look at Marilyn and think, "Gee, I'd hate to be her." In my opinion she is a glowing example of a Proverbs 31 woman. She once told me that one of her greatest achievements was in pursuing a counseling course that enabled her to help someone in trouble. The person she was "helping," looked at her in amazement and said, "How do you know all this? You are reading me like a book!" Marilyn was then able to assist this person piece her broken experience together.

Marilyn became a woman of resolve. She made herself available and she brought answers to someone in need. She found herself explaining to this lady the reason for her trouble and she possessed the necessary tools to fix the situation. Isn't that a great story? Leadership is about helping people put their lives together again. Remember the nursery rhyme, "All the king's horses and all the king's men couldn't put Humpty together again?" But you and I can, because we are not empowered by an earthly king but by the magnificent King of Heaven. Even more exciting is that, armed with the anointing of God's Spirit, we can birth big, beautiful things beyond our wildest dreams.

CHAPTER FIFTEEN

Birth Something Big and Beautiful

For a number of years I had the privilege of teaching our Partnership program. It is a simple course that quickly cements the heart and spirit of our church into the hearts of those attending our church or those that are new to our house. In my session I talked about commitment. Certain mindsets outside the kingdom of God often regard that commitment as a somewhat offensive concept. Sadly, they are mistaken because *commitment* simply means to deposit or entrust oneself to something.

As we commit to a magnificent, kind, and generous heavenly Father, we are simply positioning ourselves under His deposit. As we entrust our lives to His goodness, He then pours into us and our life expands. I totally loved explaining to all these wonderful new people how much God truly wants to increase the quality and quantity of their lives. God wants to increase, expand, and enlarge our capacity. In a funny way, He wants to increase the quantity or expansiveness of our lives so that He can spread us like "happy-dust" (or goodness) all over the earth. So many people live their lives in a small way, when God wants to release the huge potential residing in them. Isaiah 54 talks about enlarging, stretching, lengthening, sparing not, and strengthening what already exists in your life. I love the concept of capacity. Remember the words that defined *capacity*—volume, character, ability, dimension, intent, magnitude, size, aptitude, brains (Oh yes! Women with brains!), capability, cleverness, and efficiency.

Imagine saying . . .

. . . "I am a woman with volume!" Now this is not license to live in the cookie jar, but rather to love the big thing God is doing in you. When people love the sound of something, they say, "Turn up the volume" (at least in our house that's what they yell). In a loving way, God wants to turn up your volume, so your story may resound, loud and clear through the earth! (Or maybe just over the fence and down your street!)

. . . "I am a woman with character." In many ways, this is referring to qualities such as integrity, but I want to suggest a woman who is full of life and personality. I love people who exude sunshine wherever they go. Sometimes we think one has to be born that way to behave that way. Not so! I believe that if we are created in the image of an amazing, fun-to-be-around-God, then fun-to-be-around is what we should be as well. I have loud, loud, loud friends and I have soft, gentle friends, but they are all fun to be around.

. . . "I am a woman with ability." Absolutely, girl! I also believe we are created in the image of a creative God! Creative juices are within us all and we simply need to learn how to unlock them. Tune into your Creator and watch the ideas flow. His grace will then enable you to actually do it. As I have already mentioned, a decade or so ago I birthed and facilitated an annual conference called "Colour Your World." Today, thousands of women from across the planet gather at our Colour conferences in Sydney, London, and Kiev. As you can imagine, organizing anything of reasonable magnitude (let alone on three different continents!) takes a lot of work and brain power (help us, Jesus!). I remember one occasion rejoicing as our conference ended because God had been so faithful and our full expectations had been met. Two days later, as I worshiped God in a midweek service, the Holy Spirit (in what seemed like a split-second moment) allowed me to visualize the format, program, and brochure concept for the following year's conference. I could not believe how easy it was and my immediate reaction was, "Man, that certainly took the pressure off!" Mind you, one still has to facilitate the plan with hard work and diligence. Never underestimate God's ability to help you become a woman of ability, because at the end of the day, He desires you to be successful at everything you put your hand to.

. . . "I am a woman with brains." Imagine for a moment a planet full of Christian women with mega-intelligence. Cerebral chicks doing awesome things in the earth, because God came and, as it teaches in Romans 12, renewed their minds, changed their mindsets, and enlarged their capacities to think, dream and achieve! I picked up a little dictionary in my study and it so aptly said:

> **brain:** organ of convoluted nervous tissue in skull of ver-
> tebrates (that's us); centre of sensation and thought (who
> told you your brains were in your big toe?);
>
> **brain child:** a product of thought;
>
> **brainstorm:** violent, mental disturbance (do not mean to

be unkind or judgmental here, but there are some dreamy, unfocused Christians in the world who could do with a violent, mental disturbance);

brain trust: a group of experts, giving impromptu answers to questions (how funny is that, but also how true. I want to be on the brain trust!);

brainwash: to systematically replace established ideas in person's mind with new ones (they stole that from Romans 12:1–2);

brain wave: bright idea.

Sounds like God to me! Being a woman of strong resolve actually sounds like fun. I believe with all my heart that the Lord desires you to be strong, convinced of your place in life and equipped with all you need to achieve this, because He has things for you to create and birth. I believe that seeds of greatness are within us all. The key is in creating the correct environment for the seeds to surface into reality. God never leaves us alone in our endeavors. He has patterned a way for us to partner for awesome success.

PART 6

BE A WOMAN
OF STRONG
PARTNERSHIP

PARTNER

koinonia (greek) \fellowship\, n.
sharing, unity, close association, participation, partnership

be a woman of

SHIP

'... a cementing together of people that is only brought about by the Holy Spirit'

strong partnership

Stevie and Donna Crouch (Photo by Fenia Shirliff)

BABY STEVIE . . .
'future girlfriend, wife, lover,
soul mate and partner in destiny'

CHAPTER SIXTEEN

Partner with Your Own Vision

I t is essential that you partner with the vision and destiny mapped out for your life. You need a personal revelation that you as an individual have something powerful to contribute to the planet and that God has put certain things in place to help you fulfill that dream and desire. You may be single, married, divorced, or widowed. You may be a woman in leadership, or a woman coming into leadership. You may be surrounded by a wonderful family and have an incredible network of friends, or you may be someone in need of the above. You may be a believer, or you may still be a seeker. You may belong to a great church, or you may be wondering where it is that God would have you planted. Regardless of your status, God has strategies in place designed to partner in your success.

Single or Married and Loving it!

You may be a single woman reading this. If you are content in your singleness, you will agree that these days, being single does not mean that you are "left on the shelf." I know literally dozens of women who are single, active, and achieving so much in life. They are partnering with the vision of their own lives and most of these excellent women do not have time to sit around wishing they were married. They are too busy having a brilliant life!

Single, married, divorced, or widowed is not a status that affects destiny. Marriage is a powerful partnership and the Word teaches that two are better than one, however, being a woman who has experienced changed marital conditions does not negate destiny. Keep your vision alive, and allow God to redefine any situation. I would be selling you a lie if I told you that a marriage breakdown is not an interruption to the plan God has for you and your partner, but I do not believe that you have to live penalized for the rest of your days because you may have a partner who decided to exit the marriage. As you maintain a pure heart before God and as you seek to do what is right, He is well able to rearrange the plan so that you as an individual can still fulfill your purpose.

I have a friend in Sri Lanka, who as a young Australian girl, fell in love with and married a Sri Lankan man called Rohan. Brian attended Bible college with Rohan, and would always say that Rohan was truly one of the kindest and most generous people he has ever known. As a young couple, they found themselves called back to Rohan's homeland, where they planted and established a wonderful ministry. One day, as Rohan was traveling in the plantation mountains, he was gunned down by rebels. Rohan laid his life down in the pursuit of seeing the gospel shared among his people. Alison was distraught and her world momentarily fell apart, but when the shock and grief subsided, conviction and resolve compelled this awesome young woman to stand up and continue serving God in her deceased husband's homeland. The vision that knit Alison and Rohan Dissaneyeke remained alive, even after Rohan left this earth. Today she is a true hero and a woman to be honored. She has remarried, and with her new husband runs an orphanage in Sri Lanka that ministers to children who have been sexually abused.

Friends and Family

Effective leadership involves effective connection with the people in the vision. You are not a leader if you are attempting to do it all by yourself. Friends and family are, more often than not, divinely appointed partners in our lives. I could not imagine Brian and I doing what we do without such wonderful people. Brian often says, "Destiny is about being in the right place, at the right time, with the right people."

The Word declares that God's goodness should extend from generation to generation (see Ps. 145). Much of society's potential is stolen because we allow the enemy to destroy families. In the church, we must believe so that the generations after us become stronger and stronger, so that God's goodness can flow uncontained from one generation to the next. Brian and I are very aware that any wise (or foolish) decision we make will affect not only our own children but also the thousands of spiritual children who often refer to us as their spiritual mum and dad. Again, effective leadership and success hinges on our ability to not only partner with the conviction of our hearts, but also to partner with the strategically placed people alongside us in the journey.

Photo by Femia Shirliff

My beautiful FAMILY

{ FEBRUARY 2000 }

CHAPTER SEVENTEEN

Partner with the One to Whom You Said "I Do!'

I f you happen to be a married, can you still remember the day you walked down the aisle and said, "I do"? What does your marriage mean to you? What do you expect from that man of yours, and what do you as an equal partner bring to your marriage? Earlier in this book, I talked a little about partnership and mentioned the importance of being yoked together. Allow me to enlarge these thoughts.

Head in the Same Direction

The mystery of marriage is that two individuals come together and, in an act of premeditated and holy covenant, they become "one flesh." In that moment, when sacred vows are exchanged, their lives are supernaturally knit together. How then can two people who are moving and breathing as one head in different directions? It is impossible—unless they intend to end in disaster. Sadly, our divorce courts are testimony to this tragic fact.

When it comes to the gender issues of marriage and life, there is nothing sadder than seeing two people out of step with one another. It affects their happiness, their future, and the people close to them. If such friction is the result of stubbornness on the behalf of a Christian, then my prayer is that the stubborn believer will wake up and get his or her act together. If you are the innocent partner, then my advice is to be a gracious Christ-like partner and seek God's specific grace and direction for your situation. Carefully listen to His voice and be obedient, because He is more than able to give you specific keys to unlock the situation.

The other possibility is that you may be married to an unbeliever. If so, you have the awesome challenge and privilege of winning the person closest to you to the love of God. Allow patience to have its perfect work. If you are serious about your partner finding Christ, be Christ-like yourself in every way. Great wisdom is to love your husband and love your children, but to serve God. Be wise, be sensitive, be patient. God is faithful. Mix hope and faith and never waver from your dream. Picture your partner standing with you, loving God and serving Him. With faith, hope, and Jesus interceding on your behalf, it will happen, as long as you continue to contribute positively. I know it will be challenging at times, but when your strength fails, that is the time to step into His strength. Remain faithful because faithfulness always prevails.

Be Evenly (Equally) Yoked

Carry the vision together with your spouse. Brian and I pastor

Hillsong Church together. We both carry the calling, mandate, and dream; we both lie awake at night buzzing with the excitement of it all, and we are both prepared to work hard and do whatever it takes to see God have His way. Nothing within me wants to work contrary to our dream. Sometimes people ask, "How do you and Brian create this platform of partnership and respect? What causes the people not only to respond to Brian, but also to you, Bobbie?" Obviously, none of this happens overnight. Respect and authority is earned over a lifetime, and is certainly something you cannot legislate.

I cannot stand up and demand that the amazing people of Hillsong Church respect me as their Senior Pastor. I have to earn that place in their hearts and the fruit of my life has to prove that I am committed to their well-being. I choose to be active, involved, and committed. I choose to be on the front row—alive, attentive, and enthused. I choose to lead by example. I choose to love God and love them, and because of that, they trust my leadership. Brian and I are called together, but it is not a power struggle because we choose to understand the dynamic of partnership—we complement and complete one another. Not all leadership couples are the same, and some women may prefer to be the quiet supporter, but nonetheless, they are a powerful partner in the equation. Remember, no kingdom or house divided against itself will ever stand (see Luke 11:17).

Carry Your Share

The yoke is likened to a harness around the neck of two oxen, called and commissioned to plough together in life. God likens our lives to the analogy of the hardworking farmer (see 2 Tim. 2), and I believe it delights the Father's heart to see a couple laboring together to achieve their purpose. There is nothing wrong with hard work. Hopefully you are married to a wonderful man who has a healthy work ethic. If so, be a blessing to him—love him, support him, cut him a little space when he needs it, and if you have been home all day, don't legislate his share of the domestics. Encourage involvement and fairness, but do not legislate. There is nothing attractive about women (or men) who legislate life. However, if you are a working woman, then you both need to address the challenges of life in the busy lane.

How do I share the load? I choose to observe and understand the pressures on my husband's life. He has to think, create, and make big decisions every day of his life. If he appears removed or distant, it is not because he doesn't love me—he just has a lot on his mind. I have learned to understand and appreciate the weight of responsibility that he carries. I choose not to add to his burden. I will not depress you by telling you I learnt this overnight. I have been married more than thirty years and I learnt many of these lessons with pain and tears. One of the greatest days in my life was many years ago when Brian stopped sharing his dreams first with his father, and started sharing them with me. I say that with no disrespect to my father-in-law, but it was a moment of break-through in our marriage. Brian wasn't insensitive, but rather we were learning what it means to be kingdom partners.

Allow Each Other the Room for Growth and Maturity

One of the greatest enemies to marriage is immature expecta-tion. Think about it—immature or pre-mature expectation. Brides walk down the aisle and Mr. Perfect seems so perfect. Of course, Mr. Perfect possibly hasn't shown his true colors yet. If he did, his bride-to-be might possibly say, "See you later alligator, I'm not marrying you." So once the honeymoon is over, reality often sets in. Relax; it's not the end of the world. Do you seriously know anyone who got married and *wham*, life was blissfully perfect? No! No couple is perfect, especially newlyweds.

Reality bites! The sex may be great (and I pray that this sacred part of your marriage is blessed), then again, sex is often not great for many. It can be a disappointment, so be wise about growing together even in intimacy. The reality of two human hearts being knit together and actually having to live together under the same roof can be a very interesting scenario.

Allow each other space to grow and mature. Hey, when I met Brian I was captivated. I fell in love with his height, his big broad shoulders, his zany, zany perspective on life. I fell in love with his masculinity, his love for God and his strength. Shock and horror—I didn't know he had stuff in his life that God had yet to redeem. In the early days of our marriage, I remember driving across Sydney and praying, "God, why is he like this?" God replied, "Excuse me, what right have you to say to the Potter (God), why have you made the pot (Brian) thus? Daughter, I haven't finished with him yet. In fact, I've hardly begun. What I want to do is change you, Bobbie." I quickly shut up.

As God has knit us together for more than thirty years of marriage, Brian has proven to be a great husband. In the early days he allowed me space to mature. I was so shy and insecure, yet he never once put any pressure on me to be anything I was not, nor any pressure to deliver what I was unable to deliver. However, he has been sensitive to God and has at various times pushed me to new level of myself. I love him for that, because my nature had tended to be a bit timid in the past. As a church, we have always tried to do likewise with all our pastors' wives. They are free to be themselves, and the only thing we require of them is devotion and commitment to the cause of Christ and His church.

Love the things that make marriage sacred. Love and treasure sweet companionship. Guard your friendship. Your spouse should be your soul mate and your best friend. Love and treasure God-given intimacy. Love sex! It is possibly the most powerful aspect of your union. God likens His love for the church to a marriage between a man and a woman, a bride and a bridegroom. This is a powerful analogy. In the natural, a marriage is consummated by sexual intercourse. The ideal and goal is that both partners would come into the union as virgins. A hymen is broken, blood is spilled, and a blood covenant is entered into. Sex is not something that we accommodate our partners with (ho-hum). It is a powerful and almost spiritual dimension to marriage. Guard this aspect of marriage with all your heart. If this side of your marriage is suffering, then seek help. Talk to God and seek help. The enemy knows how powerful our sexuality is, because it is possibly the most sought after, corrupted target in life.

Embrace the Learning Curves Together

Laugh together, cry together, grow together! Help each other. Be strong when they are weak, and allow their strength to sustain you when you are feeling fragile. I want to be the kind of woman who can:

- encourage when she is hard pressed or stressed,
- love when she is fragile,
- listen when someone needs a sounding board, and
- be warm and available when another's soul needs a playmate.

Let's be women who truly complete the picture. Paint your marriage beautiful. You and your partner are about the only ones who can do it.

Rejoice Together in the Rewards

Life is full of blessings, but sometimes we can be so busy and consumed that we fail to recognize them. Having someone to snuggle up next to in bed is a blessing. Sitting the family down for a meal is a blessing. Having friends to share life with is a blessing. God's heart is to bless you, and His Word declares that His favor is toward His faithful children. Proverbs 8:35 says, "For whoever finds me [Wisdom] finds life and draws forth and obtains favor from the Lord" (AMPLIFIED BIBLE). Sometimes that blessing and favor expresses itself in big rewards, but usually the best rewards are the everyday things that involve friends and family.

Treasure everything. Be grateful for everything. Give thanks to your Heavenly Father for everything. God has truly blessed me. I have an exceptional husband, I have three magnificent children who constantly warm my heart, and I have friends who are so precious that it makes me want to cry. Our church is perfect, not because they are faultless but because their hearts are so willing. I love my family, I love my home, I love my church, and I love my life.

God never ceases to amaze me, but I thank Him continually for everything. I drive up to our church building and I thank God that the trees are growing beautifully. I thank God that someone has mowed the lawns. Every time I see a parking attendant, I greet them by blowing a kiss or waving. I thank God for faithful people who love the house of God as much as we do. I thank God for my garden. I cannot look at my grapevine (yes, grapevine!) without thanking God for it. I love it when it's green; I love it when it changes color; I love it when it's bare. I thank God for my carpet. Every time I lie on it and read my Bible or do my tummy-crunches (yuck, but needful these days), I thank God for my carpet. It's only carpet—it's not mink, in case some of you were wondering. I thank God for every sweet thing that comes my way, although I did struggle at times to get total victory over the volume of laundry that emerged from the bedrooms of my house when all my kids were at home. What am I trying to say here? Be thankful. Be a *thankful* person. Recognize and count your blessings—you may be surprised how blessed you are. And if you aren't feeling blessed, then go back to the beginning of this book because God needs to get through to you.

We have talked about partnering with your own vision and partnering with your husband, if you have one. There are two more partnerships I want to briefly mention.

CHAPTER EIGHTEEN

Partner with the Master Plan

R esist the temptation to do life alone. God, in His infinite wisdom, is fashioning us together into one family, one body, and one house. I have also written a book called *Heaven Is in This House,* which I believe gives expression to God's heart regarding His beautiful church. God's desire is to bring heaven to earth in and through our individual and collective lives. Vibrant, healthy churches where His people are free and empowered to flourish is part of that master plan.

Partner with the Other Limbs and Ligaments

The master plan is that we belong to and connect within the body of Christ (His church). He knows that if we do not connect, we'll be like a little limb sitting out in the middle of nowhere. The rest of the body will be about its business and there, sitting all alone and trying to make it on its own in the big wide world, will be a little finger, toe, foot or hand. Chances are, the body will continue on (perhaps a little disabled because it's missing something important—hopefully not you!) but it's very likely that those little "body bits" will wither up and die out there on their own. Of course, I am speaking about your spiritual well-being.

Partnership actually means "to share." It means to share in His love, His goodness, and His purposes. Understand that the God who knew us all before the foundations of the earth also predestined and planted us together in time and history. I often look at our gorgeous congregation and think how bizarre that God chose to plant us all together—He must have known we'd be brilliant together. Some Christians totally misunderstand this. They love God, but they incorrectly think they belong to some ethereal, universal church and can flit from here to there, feeding from anyone's table. Wrong! Of course Christians across the earth are referred to as His church or bride, but God needs us committed on the ground, making a difference in our local communities, cities, and nations.

Think of a real family, and imagine a newborn baby in the family as a newborn Christian. They come out of the delivery room (the new Christian's class) and we say, "Oh, just go wherever you want." That's like saying to a toddler, "You can eat and sleep wherever you want. Just bump into any family in the neighborhood at suppertime and . . . well, have a nice life." How stupid is that? That mindset carries no sense of accountability, stewardship, commitment, or joy in witnessing maturity. It is like being born and then orphaning yourself.

God loves His church. He likes the idea of family, of the body, and of His house. Understanding this will help you live God's best for your life.

Partner with Heaven's Go-between

Who is "heaven's go-between"? He is the beautiful and magnificent Holy Spirit. In Chapter Twelve, I mentioned how we shouldn't ignore the dynamic of the Holy Spirit and that to be women of strong conviction, resolve, and partnership, we need to recognize the power of partnering with the Spirit of God. This subject is extensive and there are countless resources you can avail yourself to, especially if you have little understanding of the Person of the Holy Spirit. God said that in the final days, He would pour out His Spirit, and the church today is growing in her revelation of this. Do not read or absorb someone's theory on the Holy Spirit. Search for a living and true understanding of this wonderful Person. The best way is to search the Scriptures with a pure and hungry heart, and I promise that God will reveal Himself.

Heaven's Holy Spirit—He is the one who hovers between heaven and earth. The Bible tells us that the Father and Son converse about us in heaven, and the Holy Spirit's job is to listen in and convey Their heart to us, so that we might be able to achieve Their will on earth. Much is being said, taught, and experienced today concerning the anointing of the Spirit. I believe the Father anoints people who seek to carry His heart, and actively perform His will upon the earth. His anointing rests upon people who love what He loves, who hate what He hates, and who pursue what is important to Him. God will anoint those who fight for what Christ died for and who are truly faithful with what He places in their hands.

All of these partnerships are designed to help us achieve maturity so we can fulfill our destinies. Maturity is a delightful concept. Maturity suggests you are ready to be released. Maturity suggests something rich, fine, and flavorsome is about to ooze from your life. Maturity suggests you might be ready to reproduce something on the earth. My prayer is that you will know who you are and all that you are purposed to achieve, that you will connect with a company of people who will partner in your success, and that the world will be a better place because of your love affair with your awesome King in heaven.

PSALM 45
ALWAYS AND FOREVER

'**color**—the many tints and hues and colorful expressions of God's goodness entering the human arena . . .'

'bella' (italian) \beautiful\
'horaios' (greek) \beautiful\
'to flourish or be at its loveliest because it has reached the right hour or season'

Dance little Princess, DANCE!

Color Your World Beautiful!

ometimes I daydream about telling the world how wonderfully magnificent God is. I imagine purchasing the front page of the city's top selling newspaper or buying the best television slot available or taking out the most spectacular spread in the most popular and glossy of magazines. Unfortunately, a world system that is unconsciously influenced by forces contrary to the goodness of God makes that difficult, however, it's not over yet and the days are coming when all this will change. In the meantime, it is up to you and me to color this beautiful planet with the goodness of God.

The Bible clearly tells us that the earth and all its fullness declare God's glory. King David recognized His handiwork and had a heart that almost exploded in his chest with love, adoration, and applause for what he saw. Both my sons are passionate about extreme sports. They love to snowboard, wakeboard, skateboard, and surf. Basically, if you can stand sideways on it, they're into it. They surf regardless of weather. One day a few years ago, Joel came home from the beach and told me he and his friends were on their boards as the sun rose. All of a sudden, they were caught in a wild electrical storm—lightning and thunder on the ocean at dawn. What more could adventure-driven teenagers hope for? He said, "Mum, it was awesome. You could feel God!"

I do understand why surfers become addicted. They love the adrenalin of the sport but they also become addicted to the dynamic of creation. God's mercies are new every morning and there is something powerful about watching a new day dawn on the earth, especially over the ocean. Right now a percentage of the planet's population may not recognize the Creator behind the new dawn, but one day they will. (By the way, my then teenage son put his order in for what he hopes heaven will be: "I'll have a very cool house—out front will be the ocean so I can surf, out back will be mountains so I can snowboard, and out the side will be a river so I can wakeboard." Keep delighting in the Lord, son, and you just might get it!) God created the earth for humanity to play in. Those of us who know and love Him are here to help this world discover the Creator behind the playground. Our responsibility is to wear Him as He is and show them what a wonderful God He really is. Sometimes unbelievers say, "Show us God. What does God look like?" My response would be, "Well, take everything in life that is wonderful, good, fabulous, creative, inviting, refreshing, fun, spontaneous, warm, generous, and humorous and you get a glimpse of God." I am sure there is an eternity more to discover, but that's a good start.

When God created the earth, His Word says it was without form, empty and void. He then released the creative genius of the Holy Spirit and the Godhead went to work. What emerged six days later was an awesome planet, perfectly put together and full of life, movement, and newness. Full of color, depth, and richness. Full of light, shade, and personality. Full of individuality. God is amazing. It never ceases to amaze me how people can walk through life and never even inquire as to who put all this together? How religion can paint such a morbid picture of Jesus and God, and how some so-called scholars can turn the Bible, a book full of promise and hope, into a negative experience never ceases to stir Brian and me.

God is life; God is color; God is everything delightful and magnificent on the earth. Now relax; this is not some new age conclusion. God is God. He is the Father, the Son, and the Holy Spirit, and I am referring to His creation, which is evidence of Him displayed throughout the earth. The Bible talks about the "manifold wisdom of God" (Eph. 3:10). The original word for *manifold* is *polupoikilos,* and it means "much varied." The Word describes God's wisdom and life as varied, with many shades, tints, hues, and colorful expressions. Let me quote the *Strong's Bible Dictionary*: "As a God of variety, He is still entering the human arena, displaying many-sided, multi-colored, and much variegated wisdom to His people and through His people" (Eph. 3: 8–10). My heart skipped a few beats when I first read this because I had just launched our women's conference and had called it "Colour Your World." How amazing to discover the conference concept wasn't just a good idea but a God idea.

Our challenge is to discover, live, and weave this color dynamic into our lives. Our challenge is then to allow the fullness of the God who lives within us to truly shine forth. God first created the playground (earth). He then created His son and daughter (Adam and Eve). They were full of potential and He loved them deeply. They ran around naked and spent their days in the garden. God Himself came, met with them in the cool of the day, and loved them. Then, one day, disobedience became their undoing. They disobeyed one simple instruction and plunged humanity into sin and separation from the Creator, Who simply longed to walk and play with them in the cool of the day. Time passed and God sent a rescue plan, which was the Law. It wasn't His perfect plan, but it would help His children stay out of trouble until the perfect plan could materialize.

In the fullness of time, God sent His only begotten Son, Jesus Christ, to stand in the gap and redeem us home. He shed His priceless blood, went to hell, took our place in a lost eternity and suffered the ultimate heartache (separation from the Father) to purchase the gift of life for humanity. Once again, God could fellowship and play with us in the cool of the day. The church exploded because Jesus rose victorious over death and destruction. Life was on the planet again and salvation's plan emerged. Yet alas, unredeemed man made a mess of it yet again, and then painted his own picture of God. Man pushed God out of His own house and empty religion took over. Thank God that lifeless religion is declining, but the church of Jesus Christ, as it ought to be, is rising on the planet. God has always kept His church alive throughout the ages, but today we are granted the privilege of experiencing an unprecedented outpouring of His Spirit.

In the last days, according to the book of Joel, He promised He would pour out His Spirit and a youth generation would catch the fire and spread the reality of a living, dynamic, and loving God. This is happening on the planet and I rejoice to be part of it. But the verses do not end there. The promise was to the older generation as well. Something wonderful is happening. Nowhere in the world do you have the generations coming together in such unity. Nowhere but in the church do you have youth dancing and rejoicing and joining vision with an older generation. Nowhere but in the church can complete strangers walk through doors for the first time and genuinely be welcomed as if they were long-lost family.

This is happening in the church of Jesus Christ today. It is happening across the nations. It transcends denomination and culture, and it is the Spirit of the Living God hovering, creating, and birthing His eternal purposes on the earth! Darkness and sadness may still run unrestrained in certain places, but as God's light emerges on His people, darkness will be dispelled. I want to encourage you. I want to exhort you. I want to place my hands on your beautiful face and say, "Rise up, woman of God." Rise up, fall in love with your Creator, get over what contains you, discover your purpose, and start coloring your world with the love of God. "Oh, taste and see that the Lord is good" (Ps. 34:8)!

Let Jesus Christ consume you. Let Him be in your life, your mouth, your dance, your step. Let Him shine forth. Allow His countenance to be your countenance and may all who taste your life, and may all who observe your sweet face, look and say, "I want what she has. I want to know this Person who brings light and love, laughter and depth to this girl. I'll have what she's having!!"

My deepest prayer is that God's smile will be upon you. I pray blessing and increase upon you and trust that one day we will meet and exchange stories.

Always and forever,
Bobbie

About the Author

With a contagious zest for life, Bobbie passionately believes in the potential of all people and is devoted to the cause of Christ. She and her husband Brian are the founders and Senior Pastors of Hillsong Church, and have an all-consuming desire to place value on humanity. To that end, they labor to see healthy men, women, and youth emerge across the landscape of the church.

Bobbie's warm personality, fresh vitality, down-to-earth good humor, and genuine love for God and His Word have helped her connect with countless people across the planet.

She is a wife, mother, friend, pastor, creative visionary, communicator, author, role model, and mentor. Her life reflects the message she teaches—that people have incredible God-given potential waiting to be unleashed. It is this message that has defined her life.

Born and raised in Auckland, New Zealand, Bobbie made the decision to follow Jesus at the age of fifteen. She's never looked back. A year after they married, Brian and Bobbie moved to Sydney,

Australia in 1978, and started what is today Hillsong Church in a small school hall in 1983. Now recognized as Australia's largest local church, Hillsong has a growing congregation with more than twenty thousand people and comprises two campuses (City and Hills), a citywide network of connect groups, extension services across the city (including a range of culturally specific services), and growing congregations in London, Kiev, and Paris.

Bobbie's desire to see value placed on womanhood is a passion that underpins the Colour Your World Women's Conference, which she hosts in Sydney, London, and Kiev annually. Since 1987, Colour has been bringing a message of value, worth, and dignity to women from around the world, encouraging and inspiring them to be all God has created them to be. Colour has also been a catalyst for mobilizing thousands of women, moved with compassion and a heart for justice, to help poor and marginalized children and women in developing nations.

Brian and Bobbie and their three grown children—Joel, Ben, and Laura—all live in Sydney, Australia.